BEAVERBROOK

A study of Max the unknown

By the same author

INNOCENT MEN
FIGHTERS EVER
IDEAS HAVE LEGS
THAT MAN FRANK BUCHMAN
MEN ON TRIAL
THE WORLD REBUILT
REMAKING MEN
AN IDEA TO WIN THE WORLD
EFFECTIVE STATESMANSHIP
AMERICA NEEDS AN IDEOLOGY
FRANK BUCHMAN'S SECRET
BRITAIN AND THE BEAST
DESIGN FOR DEDICATION

Plays

THE REAL NEWS
THE DICTATORS' SLIPPERS
THE BOSS
WE ARE TOMORROW
THE VANISHING ISLAND
RUMPELSNITS
THE MAN WHO WOULD NOT DIE
MIRACLE IN THE SUN
PICKLE HILL
THE HURRICANE
THE LADDER
MUSIC AT MIDNIGHT
SPACE IS SO STARTLING
THROUGH THE GARDEN WALL
THE DIPLOMATS
MR. BROWN COMES DOWN THE HILL

BEAVERBROOK

A study of Max the unknown

PETER HOWARD

HUTCHINSON OF LONDON

HUTCHINSON & CO. (*Publishers*) LTD
178–202 Great Portland Street, London W1

London Melbourne Sydney
Auckland Bombay Toronto
Johannesburg New York

First published 1964
Reprinted before publication

This book has been set in Bembo, printed in Great Britain on Antique Wove paper by The Anchor Press, Ltd., and bound by Wm. Brendon & Son Ltd., both of Tiptree, Essex.

CONTENTS

1
BLACK INK
Beaverbrook the Battleground
9

2
FEARS AND FOES
Beaverbrook the Man
12

3
FAITHS AND FAMILY
Beaverbrook the Idealist
29

4
DESTINY AND DISAPPOINTMENT
Beaverbrook the Politician
39

5
PEERAGE AND PRESS
Beaverbrook the Newspaperman
59

6
MAX B., STANLEY B.
Beaverbrook the Enemy
71

7
BELOW THE BELT
Beaverbrook the Boxer
83

8

TROUBLE IN PARADISE

Beaverbrook the Friend

93

9

WAR AND AWARENESS

Beaverbrook the Peacemaker

105

10

PROPAGANDA AND PROPHECY

Beaverbrook the Prophet

117

11

MACHINES AND MAGIC

Beaverbrook the Patriot

123

12

MAX AND THE MONARCHY

Beaverbrook the Subject

136

13

BEHAVIOUR AND BELIEF

Beaverbrook the Christian

143

14

STEEL AND STRAW

Beaverbrook the Total

152

15

EPILOGUE

162

ACKNOWLEDGEMENTS

Grateful acknowledgements are made to the authors and publishers for permission to quote extracts from the following books: *My War Memories*, by General E. von Ludendorff (Hutchinson & Co. (Publishers) Ltd.); *History of the English People in the Nineteenth Century*, Volume V, by E. Halévy (Ernest Benn Ltd.); *Down the Years*, by Sir Austen Chamberlain (Cassell & Company Ltd.); *King George V*, by Sir Harold Nicolson (Constable & Co. Ltd.); *Lord Derby, 'King of Lancashire'*, by Randolph Churchill (William Heinemann Ltd.); *The Londoner*, by Tudor Jenkins (MacGibbon & Kee Ltd.); *Baldwin's Age*, edited by John Raymond (the extract quoted is taken from an essay by Francis Williams) (Eyre & Spottiswoode (Publishers) Ltd.); *Sacred Songs and Solos*, No. 274, by Ira D. Sankey (Marshall, Morgan & Scott); *The Mist Procession*, by Lord Vansittart (Hutchinson & Co. (Publishers) Ltd.); *A Diary with Letters, 1931–1950*, by Thomas Jones (Oxford University Press), and *Stanley Baldwin, Man or Miracle?*, by Bechover Roberts (Robert Hale & Co. Ltd.).

Thanks are also due to the Executors of the late Lord Beaverbrook for permission to quote from books by Lord Beaverbrook: *The Divine Propagandist, Politicians and the War, 1914–1916, Politicians and the Press*, and *Friends*. Also to The Beaverbrook Foundations for permission to quote from *War Memoirs of David Lloyd George*, Volume II.

1

BLACK INK

Beaverbrook the Battleground

I WAS at war with Lord Beaverbrook.

I was at war with him for years. It was a battle without blood though not without tears, sweat, and a gale or two of laughter. There could be no end to the struggle save unconditional surrender. It was his money or his life—his success or his soul—the *Daily Express* or the Everlasting Mercy.

Beaverbrook showed small disposition to yield. For my part, I dared not abate. He had the power, the glory, and a thousand sharp swords to his command. I had only the pinprick of a persistence that would not be denied and a vision for the man far wider than his own massive achievement.

Many years ago Augustine Birrell, who was the son of a Baptist minister, said to Beaverbrook, 'Young man, you have fine ability and a first-rate knowledge of people. You will live to do a great deal of mischief.' The son of the Baptist was accurate in his prediction about the son of the Scottish Presbyterian manse.

There is an old legend of a man rich in every human quality. His wit was like diamonds. His wealth as the sands of the sea. His charm so true that husbands called him the best of good fellows while wives sadly and secretly compared him with their menfolk in their hearts. He could have been the great moralist of his generation—even the Archbishop of Canterbury had he believed in the Episcopacy, or perhaps the editor of the *Guardian*.

But there was another side to his character. It was the devil with two sticks. Part of him was brilliant with wickedness and guile—swift to expose, eager to believe the worst, and with a charm so honey-like that husbands cursed him, and wives said there was no comparison with their husbands at all, at all.

Warfare for this man of the legend never ended. Many took part in the struggle. Would he become the mighty moral force of his day? Or would he go the way of the devil with two sticks? Sadly the story records that the devil came away with victory perched on his brimstone banners.

And in the case of Beaverbrook, the devil with two sticks was the circulation of the *Daily Express*. He worshipped that vast and growing circulation, not for the sake of money but for the sake of propaganda. His propaganda was in favour of the British Empire which seemed to appeal more to him than the propagation of the Kingdom of God.

My task is not to blame Beaverbrook nor to praise him. I scorn toadies who tumble each other out of their tracks as they rush to lick the boots of the powerful. I spew from my lips those who have not done and never will do one-tenth of what Beaverbrook did for himself and our country, but who snarled and sneered at him from positions of superiority that were self-appointed and silly.

I wanted nothing from the man for myself but demanded one thing from him for the sake of us all. That was that he don the mantle of a greater greatness that should have been his and which he sturdily refused to cast around his shoulders.

Beaverbrook once declared that if he had his time again he would be an evangelist, a man who preached the gospel as his father, with long, white beard and deep-set eyes, preached it to the citizens of New Brunswick. That will and heart and brain which won millions of readers for the *Daily Express* could surely have won enough souls in Britain to have altered the course and character of the land. Beaverbrook could and should have used his shining skills, untarnished to the last, and the magic of his mind undimmed to do what he knew he should have been doing all along.

It is not for man to judge men. Yet it was possible to believe that unless this war for Beaverbrook were won, then a life which seemed so full of triumph in the eyes of humanity might be a tragedy in the eyes of Heaven—the tragedy of one of the great men of our century who chose a lesser path, whose moral comprehensions were not fully matched by his mortal conduct, who preferred the comfort of compromise to the Cross, the black ink of Fleet Street to the red blood of Calvary.

It could be the sad tale of a genius who put flesh before faith, human desires before divine destiny, the circulation of the *Daily Express* before the moral and spiritual rearmament of Commonwealth and world.

No doubt when we meet our Maker face to face, we are in for some surprises. Those who seem saintly on earth may find themselves spottier than their reputation. While those who seized life by the throat with both hands and shook it rudely, gladly, violently, may find they have accomplished more in the mind of God than a legion of prim, prudish prodnoses. Some of those who drained life's flagon until its bottom was up may have surpassed the negative host of upturned noses.

Be that as it may, war with Beaverbrook went on. Not for my sake. Not even for his sake. But for the sake of millions whose lives would have been touched by a miracle in the life of that human maelstrom. The trumpets of Heaven can yet sound loud enough to drown the thunder of those Fleet Street machines that roared in the ears of the lord of the Inky Art. And his press could be a powerful prophet for a Britain renewed in strength of character and faith.

2

FEARS AND FOES

Beaverbrook the Man

THIS is a portrait of a friend. It is neither a photograph nor an X-ray picture. It is not an attempt to tell the whole story of a life, inside or out. Between these covers I paint on broad canvas the outlines I see, as I see them, of my friend William Maxwell Aitken, born 25 May 1879 in Maple, Ontario, Canada, and afterwards called Lord Beaverbrook.

I knew him upwards of thirty years.

Friendship is like port wine. Age ripens both. Time's secret magic eases acid from wine and brings to mellowness and maturity the taste of sunshine seasons of long ago.

Friendship, like wine, can sometimes give you a headache. Friends do not always behave in just the way you think they should. But true friendship does not depend on mere agreement.

Friendship is something that can ever be given, but seldom earned. Indeed, few things in life are so irksome as a man who circles around you like a bean round a pole or a dog round a lamp-post, wishing to earn your favour and to use you for his purposes. It is lucky for most of us that friendship does not depend solely on each other's virtues. Otherwise, most of us would have few friends.

My portrait is that of a man of courage and of character too, unafraid. It is a view of a man whose head so brimmed with brains that it aroused the sneers and suspicions of the dullards; whose heart was large enough to love this country better than many of those who were born in it; and whose hand was in the habit of being bitten by those it had fed.

Some painters coax character on to canvas. They find venom in a Venus and mercy in a Mars. As I begin this portrait of a friend, the story comes to memory of a provincial mayor who had his picture painted. He said to another man, 'I hope the artist does me justice'. This man, after looking at the mayor with care, answered, 'It is not justice you need. It is mercy.'

Max Beaverbrook needs no mercy from me. I am prejudiced about him. Not only did I like him. But I am convinced that when the shifting kaleidoscope of our times, coloured by boot-licking, backbiting, feuds and gossip, jealousy and hate, satire and hypocrisy, steadies into the clear perspective of history, Beaverbrook will be seen as a giant of his times. Sometimes wicked, sometimes good—but in a mighty mould. Some stand too close to grasp his stature. One of his staff said not long ago, 'He is the last of the great pirates—a brigand of our times'.

Max was a man. He was a magician with money. But he was more than that. He was a master of the black art of ink. But he was more than that. Those who downed champagne in his home and downed his character when they left it, missed the mark when they called him a mischief-maker (though he made much mischief) and talked about 'that old devil Max' (though devilry was an ingredient in the cocktail of his character).

In two great wars this century, Beaverbrook played a patriot's part in saving the life of Britain. And two great fighting men, one German, one British, can give their evidence.

General Eric von Ludendorff, in the book called *My War Memories*, giving his account of World War I, says this: 'We [the Germans] were hypnotized by the enemy propaganda as a rabbit is by a snake. It was exceptionally clever and conceived on a great scale. It worked by strong mass-suggestion, kept in the closest touch with the military situation, and was unscrupulous as to the means it used. . . . While Entente propaganda was doing ever more harm to the German people and the army and navy, it succeeded in maintaining the determination to fight in its own countries and armies and in working against us in neutral countries. . . . In the neutral countries we were subject to a sort of moral blockade. In England the whole propaganda service was placed under Lord Beaverbrook.' (Under his direction, Lord Northcliffe was responsible for propaganda in enemy countries, Rudyard Kipling for home and colonial propaganda, and, later, Lord Rothermere for the neutral countries.)

Of World War II, Sir Hugh Dowding, Commander-in-Chief of Britain's Fighter Command during the Battle of Britain, said, 'The effect of the appointment of Lord Beaverbrook to the post of Minister of Aircraft Production can only be described as magical, and thereafter the supply position improved to such a degree that the heavy aircraft wastage which was later incurred during the Battle of Britain ceased to be the primary danger, its place being taken by the difficulty of providing trained fighter pilots in adequate numbers'.

Beaverbrook described himself as a 'propagandist'. The old-style word for that is 'prophet'. And Beaverbrook was a prophet not without honour among those who understand the march of man in this troubled century.

As a candidate for honour he had, of course, serious handicaps. In the book of Job it says, 'O that mine adversary had written a book'. The modern man would say, 'O that mine adversary were a publisher of newspapers'. Such people need no candle. They live in the glare all their lives.

Each day news, views, pictures, scandals, attacks—all the glitter, gunpowder, and razzle-dazzle of the Press—lands on millions of breakfast-tables. In their time cartoonists like Low, acid-slingers like Michael Foot, men with pens dipped in salt and sugar, treacle and tar have had the run of the *Express*. Beaverbrook was held responsible for them all. No matter what he might say, anyone who objected to anything in any of Beaverbrook's newspapers (and it is fair to add that through years a number of people have objected) blamed Beaverbrook. And in a sense they were justified in doing so.

A mistake of ill-judgement, or ill-temper, made in private, or even in public, is speedily denied or soon forgotten. The printed word is lasting and undeniable. A man so intensely powerful should also appear to the public as intensely just. But his newspapers have not always appeared intensely just. Beaverbrook has been condemned by his critics on that account. Men like him, who stride always in the thick of human conflict, are surrounded by those who will knife them if they stumble. But if some of his critics offered Beaverbrook the justice they demanded from him, they would see a truer picture of the man.

Another handicap was his background. Do not mistake me. He was sprung from centuries of Scottish soil. His forebears earned bread with the sweat of their brow. It is the most honourable ancestry a man can boast. His grandfather was Robert Aitken, of Silver Mine, Torpichen, Linlithgowshire, a gardener.

> Oh, Adam was a gardener, and God Who made him sees
> That half a proper gardener's work is done upon his knees.

Beaverbrook's father was the first of the family to lift himself by the exertions of his education from the tilts of the plough, the heft of the spade, and the whipple-tree of the harrows. The Rev. William Cuthbert Aitken went to Canada as a Minister of the Church of Scotland.

When he reached his early twenties, Max, the son of the manse, had made a fortune. He came to England rich and became richer. This was an unpopular thing to do at a time when many gilded birds of paradise, born rich through no effort of their own, had their golden tail-feathers rudely plucked from them by the turmoil of a revolutionary century and of two Great Wars. Some of the old rich families were apt to resent a man who, while they were moulting, had grown a fine crop of feathers; a man who, while their fortunes fell, by his own efforts rose to vast wealth.

Success is seldom popular with the unsuccessful. And many a snob who failed, eased his feelings by sneering at Lord Beaverbrook's background. I am bound to say Lord Beaverbrook did not make it any easier for this kind of person by his attitude to them. He was by nature an 'aginner' and particularly agin the nobs and snobs of the world whom he both scorned and envied.

One night at dinner a young and beautiful woman sat at his table. She was an actress. Among the other guests were some well-known and well-born people. Beaverbrook aimed to set the actress at her ease by poking fun at the aristocracy. He mocked their quirks and foibles. He did it with ability and agility. Barb after barb sank into the blubber of the well-born whales and social sharks who gurgled and puffed in his private ocean that night. The actress munched on. She said nothing. Finally, Beaverbrook turned and asked her, 'What do you think of all this?' She put down her knife and fork and said, 'Well, if you must know, I think you joined the club of your own accord. They did not ask you.' Then she went on with her food.

She was referring to his acceptance of a peerage as a reward for his services in pulling Asquith down and setting Lloyd George up as Prime Minister of Britain in the First World War.

It is a custom in Parliament for a man to declare his interest in a subject before he speaks about it. So I now declare my interest in Beaverbrook. I met him by chance. I was employed by him for seven years. He was in the War Cabinet when issues arose in the *Express* which led to my withdrawal. We corresponded, and from time to time I was his guest at Cherkley or Cap d'Ail. His papers have often attacked myself and my friends—as I believe unfairly. But he gave me my start in life and I remain grateful.

As a young man, I was married and poor. A friend of mine, who worked on the *Express*, took me one evening to a club called the Empire Crusade Club. People there spoke about Empire Free Trade and Splendid Isolation. All seemed to favour it. Some were fatuous in their favouritism. I rose to my feet and said so. To my astonishment, when the meeting ended, a short, vigorous man whose head seemed too heavy for his body, whose eyes stuck into me like skewers, came up, shook my hand and said with a Canadian accent, 'Mr. Howard, my best congratulations. I have listened to all you had to say tonight with closest attention. And it will all be in tomorrow's *Daily Express*.' In fact, it appeared next afternoon in the *Evening Standard*.

It must be said that Lord Beaverbrook wore his Canadian accent with the pride with which a woman wears a mink coat. Once he was saying at dinner, 'You might write an article on accents. Lord Curzon—the late and great—used to pronounce words like "dance" as if they rhymed with "pants". Then you can say of Lord Beaverbrook that he always calls the horse race the *Durby* except when he remembers to call it the *Darby*.' A lady, a good friend of his, broke in to say, 'You will be far more accurate if you write that he always calls it the *Darby* except when he remembers to call it the *Durby*'.

Two weeks after my first meeting with Beaverbrook I had a telephone call asking me to go and see him. I went. As soon as I entered the room, he said to me, 'I hear you are going to write a political article for me, Howard?' This was the first I knew of it. But for seven rich years I sat at his feet and wrote articles on politics, society, the Empire, tobacco, pubs, and every subject on earth.

The training I had was beyond price. The truth is, if I paid back all I earned (alas, it is spent long since) that sum never could buy what Beaverbrook gave me. Every word of almost every article I wrote was chewed, swallowed, or spewed forth in disgust by that hungry and discriminating jaw. He would read through some effort, scanning it slowly and carefully. Then a dialogue something like this would take place:

Lord B.: Did you do this all by yourself?
P.H. (puffing with pride): Yes.
Lord B.: Did you write every word of it yourself without getting help from anyone at all?
P.H.: Yes.
Lord B. (scrumpling up the papers and throwing them on the floor): I can't believe it of you, Peter. It's so bad. Now there's a typewriter in the other room. Go outside and do it all over again.

From his criticisms I learned to create. But he overdid criticism in his newspapers. Every comma was scanned. Every colon was scrutinized. Every word was weighed. And much of it was wasted effort. It was, as someone once said, 'So damned detailed that it dams the flow'. Beaverbrook had to have his pen in every inkpot inside the *Daily Express*.

He said in recent years that he was not enough in touch with his staff. This view was not shared by all those, especially the executives, who worked on his newspapers. But it is true that, though a circle of intimates remained, fewer of his men knew Beaverbrook than knew him years ago.

When I worked with him, his praise was lavish. His blame no less so. Sometimes I thought of him as Santa Claus, sometimes as Satan. Sometimes it was Christmas, sometimes the Day of Judgement. Though you were often conscious of being a goose, he had the encouraging and endearing habit of always expecting you to lay a golden egg. It is true of life that if somebody expects the best of you, you can sometimes rise to it.

He had his friends. He had his foes. If you worked with him, it was wise to know which was which. Remorseless in revenge if somebody attacked him, or betrayed causes to which he gave his allegiance, at no time did I see him hit someone when they were down, or unless he had been first provoked.

Then, if my friendships break and bend,
There's little need to cry,
The while I know that every foe
Is faithful till I die.

In the days when he and Baldwin were at each other's underbellies, complaints about what I had written would sometimes come by telephone from Sir Samuel Hoare, later Lord Templewood, who was a friend of both B.s. I happened to be in the room when Hoare called Beaverbrook. *Beaverbrook:* 'Yaas . . . Yaas . . . Yaas. . . . Now listen to me. I can't do anything with the fellow. No. I tell you I can't do anything with him. Now, listen. . . . Listen. I tell you what I'll do. I'll have him here and I'll roll him in the mud. Yaas. I'll roll him in the mud. Will that satisfy you?. . . . Good-bye to you.'

Then, replacing the telephone, he looked at me and a grin like a slice of melon cut across his face. He began to slap his hands on his knees and to laugh. 'Ha, ha, ha. Do it again next week, Peter. Do it again next week.'

And indeed, I did.

When Randolph Churchill, in his hey-day of youthful politics, was fighting Malcolm MacDonald in a by-election, Beaverbrook backed Randolph. William Barkley, then, as now, one of the wittiest political writers in the game, was sent to the constituency. His reports delighted everybody except Randolph who thought they gave too much space to Barkley and too little to Churchill. Randolph unwisely complained to Barkley who came straight back to Fleet Street.

Later that night I was working with Beaverbrook when Randolph telephoned. It was clear that he was complaining about Barkley. If I had had the chance, I could have told Randolph this was a mistake.

For nearly five minutes Randolph made a Churchillian oration at the other end of the line. Every now and again Beaverbrook said, 'Yaas'. When at last there was silence,

Beaverbrook said, 'Have you finished? Is that all, Randolph? Now, you just listen to me. I've been on the end of this line for some time while you've talked to me. I'm getting old. The older I get the deafer I get. I've tried to listen to you with the closest attention, but I haven't heard one word you've said to me. AND IT'S DAMNED LUCKY FOR YOU I HAVEN'T. Good-bye to you.'

At all hours of day and night, my telephone bell would ring. Sometimes at two o'clock in the morning I would hear that tough Canadian voice, 'Peter? You're a young man and it's just the time to be up and working. Now get out of bed, there's a good boy. Put on your clothes. Get to it. We need an article for today's *Evening Standard*.'

Soon after I began to work with him, Beaverbrook gave me this piece of advice. 'Never apologize, Peter, Never say sorry. Never admit you have been wrong.'

Few men have spoken in life to me so roughly as Beaverbrook. None has, at times, said sorry with more grace and space. And though employed by him, I was treated by him as a son of the house when in his home. Yet the storm-clouds could gather fast. More than once I have been grimly ordered out of the place when my views were different from his own.

When King Edward VIII, now the Duke of Windsor, was on the throne and wishing to wed Mrs. Simpson and remain as King, it was bold to tell Beaverbrook that the plan was brave but bogus—that it could never work. When the local inhabitants began chalking rude messages about the American lady on the walls of the Highland stations, Beaverbrook did not want to hear it. He ordered me out of his house for telling him I did not believe the King could wed the lady and keep his throne.

Once, when I was ill, Beaverbrook wanted an article from me. I crawled out of bed and did it. It stank in his nostrils. Even the commas displeased him. With growls of thunder and flashes of lightning he drove me forth into the street. As I walked away I heard the scurry and patter of slippered steps on the pavement behind me. I turned. There was Beaverbrook. 'I'm sorry, Peter,' he panted, 'I should never have spoken that way to you. Will you forgive me?' He possessed the genius of planting his boot in your pants and at the same time playing a tune with his hand on your heart-strings.

Another time I had a badly infected, impacted wisdom tooth. It was hauled out of my jaw with heaves and crunches. As I lay in bed recovering, my telephone rang. It was Beaverbrook who, as soon as he heard my condition, said, 'Good-bye to you', and rang off. Half an hour later, someone came to the door of my London house. Frail and ill, I opened it. There stood Albert, Beaverbrook's valet, in one hand a flask of hot soup (the last thing in the world I would or could swallow), on the other arm a sheaf of flowers so splendid and costly that if someone sent them to my funeral, my ghost would haunt them for extravagance.

Albert came in and, sitting down, said, 'The Lord has sent me'. (Albert always called his master 'The Lord'.) 'I am going to wait here till Mrs. Howard arrives.' I told him that as my wife was with the children in the country for several days he was in for a long wait. 'She'll be here soon', said Albert. 'The Lord telephoned to her.' Sure enough, an hour or two later my wife arrived. Beaverbrook had telephoned saying I was ill in bed and needed her at my side. He scolded her for her absence. She drove too fast from Suffolk, imagining I was dead or dying.

It was this same Albert, cynical but kindly, loyal but sharp, who assured Pressmen if they came late at night through the hospitable doors of Stornoway House, 'Watch them lions, sir. Every time a virgin goes past them they wink.'

The lions guarded the foot of the stairway and were carved in wood.

Albert had a wicked sense of humour. He was not restricted by accuracy in his judgements. The flower of Britain's beauty and her virtue were among those who came to Beaverbrook's home. They mingled with the well-known men and women of the country drinking with their host upstairs, members of Government and Opposition, Trade Union leaders and businessmen, writers, artists, film stars, and Pressmen. But if anyone asked Albert who was there, Albert would reply, 'Parasites and prostitutes'. It was meant as nothing but a joke. Yet it is true that Beaverbrook was at his best in the company of sinners rather than of saints. Maybe he found them easier to believe in. Certainly there are more of them in the modern world, which is one reason why so many people claimed Beaverbrook's friendship.

When first I went to work for him somebody who knew him well said to me, 'If you want to get on with Max, have trouble with the police, fall into debt, or go off with another woman'. The joke was not meant with full seriousness. But if I had got into trouble there were few men to whom I would so readily have turned as Beaverbrook.

In his book, *The Divine Propagandist*, he says, 'I am filled with a sense of utter unworthiness'. I accept that as the truth. And just as a drunkard can feel more at home with men holding tankards or glasses in their hands, so a man with a sense of unworthiness may feel more at ease with those who neither look too good, nor talk too wise. Indeed, most of us do.

Beaverbrook knew the Bible. If you heard him and saw him acting the stories of the Old Testament, you never could forget them. He told the story of Samson in such a way that you looked with fresh eyes at every woman you met. His grim account of how Haman planned to kill Mordecai, the Jew, but how instead Haman was humbled and hanged on the gallows prepared for Mordecai, made your neck twitch.

And his story of how Micaiah, the prophet, in spite of the smooth promises of the sycophants and boot-lickers at the court of King Ahab, dared to tell that monarch the truth and predict disaster to the realm, made you almost believe Beaverbrook when he said, 'I want men around me who will tell me exactly what they think, whether I agree or disagree'. It is fair to say that he had too few of them.

Sometimes in the evenings he could be persuaded to sing. He favoured old hymns and songs of tradition and ribaldry. The hymns meant most to him. Not long ago I came upon him walking on the grass at sunset. A friend walked by his side. As the gold of the evening poured over the dark yew forest, he sang in a strong voice:

'I fear no foe.'

Then he said, 'That's my motto in life, Peter'.

Again he sang:

'I fear no foe with Thee at hand to bless;
Ills have no weight, and tears no bitterness;
Where is death's sting? Where, Grave, thy victory?
I triumph still, if Thou abide with me.'

He had a sense of humour which enabled him to laugh even at himself—provided he made the jokes. Valentine Castlerosse, the Irish peer who wrote a sharp, glittering column for many years called *Londoner's Log*, was his choice companion. Once Castlerosse decided to get married. In fact he decided twice to do so, but this was the first time.

John Gordon, at that time editor of the *Sunday Express*, told Beaverbrook that Doris Delavigne (later the first Lady Castlerosse) had taken out a licence to marry Castlerosse. He believed the wedding was to be on the next day.

Beaverbrook at once telephoned Castlerosse and invited him to come with him to the South of France at 9 o'clock next morning. Castlerosse agreed. The marriage was put off.

In the South of France, Beaverbrook and Castlerosse golfed together and sat in the sun. They wined and dined.

After several days, Whelan, Beaverbrook's secretary,

discovered on the bills that his master was being asked to pay the charge for a bottle of champagne sent each afternoon to an hotel bedroom in Cannes. He made enquiries. He found that Doris Delavigne had followed Castlerosse to Cannes and that Castlerosse was sending her champagne each day and charging it to Beaverbrook.

Beaverbrook demanded that the lady leave the country at once. Otherwise he would return to London taking Castlerosse with him. Castlerosse said, 'She will go'.

Next day Beaverbrook received a letter from the lady, who had travelled as far as Monte Carlo, and wrote, 'My Lord, a woman's bed is her castle'.

Castlerosse spent money like air. The good Lord provides air, but Lord Beaverbrook had to provide money. Often Beaverbrook paid Castlerosse's gambling debts. Once Castlerosse came out of the St. James's Club with Lord Queensberry. He said to Queensberry, 'Don't tell Max. It would be bad for his health.' He knew he would have to come to Beaverbrook for the money and wanted to be first to break the news to him.

Finally Beaverbrook's patience was exhausted. He bolted the door and barred the window against Castlerosse. For some weeks he saw nothing of him. Instead Captain Mike Wardell, then employed on the *Evening Standard* and now a successful publisher in Canada, consorted with him.

Freddy Lonsdale, the playwright, who knew this situation well, found himself sitting next to Castlerosse at dinner, and with some malice asked, 'And how is Max?' Castlerosse instantly replied, 'Didn't you know? He's in gaol.' As Lonsdale had lunched with Beaverbrook that day, this news surprised him. He asked what had happened. 'Well,' said Castlerosse, 'you may have heard that he's been seeing a lot of Wardell lately. Last night they were dining together. Wardell talked before dinner. He talked all through the first course. He talked all through the second course. He went on talking. Finally, when wine was being served, Max picked up a bottle and smashed it on Wardell's head. I think he killed him. Then he rang the bell for Albert and shouted, "Take away the corpse and send for Castlerosse". So they had to lock him up.'

Lonsdale at once went to Beaverbrook and repeated this story to him. Beaverbrook roared with laughter and next day Castlerosse was back at his table again.

Castlerosse was a royal jester. He died with a joke at the end of his pen. An industrialist, a friend of Lord Beaverbrook, was held up at Shannon airport on his way to Canada. He telephoned Castlerosse who at once fetched him to Killarney and took him on a round of golf.

Castlerosse at this time had been warned by doctors to cut down his drinking. He was allowed two whiskies a day. But there were a number of huts on the golf-course he had built at Killarney. They were locked. Castlerosse held the key. And in each hut was whisky.

Castlerosse and the industrialist, also well known for his love of the bottle, visited every hut as they played their golf. At the end of the round Castlerosse returned home and said to his wife, 'Darling, I've been a good boy. Can I have one of my whiskies?' His wife carefully measured him his drink.

Castlerosse took the industrialist to Shannon and put him on the plane to Canada. He then wrote to Beaverbrook, 'When your friend gets to Canada he will read many advertisements telling him, "Drink Canada Dry". From what I have seen of him here, I'm afraid he may take this as a challenge.'

By the time this letter reached Beaverbrook, Castlerosse was dead.

Tim Healy was a dear friend of Beaverbrook. He was the first Governor-General of the Irish Free State, brilliant Parliamentarian, devout Catholic.

He was waiting at the waterfront near Dublin one day when Beaverbrook arrived in his yacht. Beaverbrook was sad. He had promised the mother of Lord Castlerosse that her son would not marry. Castlerosse had promised his mother the same thing. But now he was wed.

Tim Healy's first words to Beaverbrook were, 'Is Valentine married?'

Beaverbrook said, 'Yes'.

'Who is the lady?' asked Tim. Beaverbrook replied with three words. Even in these days they are not words to print. But they implied that the lady loved freely, loved money, and was not loved by him.

Tim Healy said, 'Is she a Catholic?' Beaverbrook nodded. Tim flung his arms to heaven and shouted, 'Glory be to God'.

On another occasion, when Asquith was Prime Minister, fighting broke out in Ireland. It became known as the 'Easter Rebellion'. Bonar Law, as Colonial Secretary and leader of the Tory Party, had to answer questions in Parliament about it. He begged Beaverbrook to telephone Healy and find out the facts. So you had the strange event of a leading Member of the British Cabinet seeking from a man on the other side of the barricades how to reply to critics in the House of Commons.

Telephone lines had been cut. Communication was difficult. At last from a telephone in the Colonial Office Beaverbrook reached Healy in Ireland. He asked, 'When did this rebellion begin?' Healy replied, 'When Strongbow came to Ireland'.

'That's all very well,' said Beaverbrook, 'but when is it going to end?' 'When Cromwell gets out of hell', answered the Irishman.

Beaverbrook was temperate. Some years ago he gave up alcohol for a time. Later, he drank whisky and champagne. He had a cellar of wine that was the envy of his friends. His food was simple but perfect. The cooking at his table was for years some of the best in Britain.

Afflicted with asthma, he gave up smoking. But he was very generous in all forms of hospitality. Sometimes this generosity got him into trouble. He once entertained the staff of one of his newspapers to a dinner-party. One man died in the taxi on the way home. He died of cancer. Another cut his arm badly and went to St. George's Hospital for the night. A third, driving with abandon along the Thames Embankment in the early hours of the morning, hit an ambulance. He was arrested by the police. He was carried off to the police station. He said to them, 'You'd better let me out of here. I've been dining with Lord Beaverbrook. If you don't let me out, he'll come here and tear the building down brick by brick.' Next day the doctor, giving evidence as to the condition of the prisoner, said, 'He told me he had been dining with Lord Willoughby de Broke'. The prisoner shouted from the dock, 'No. Lord Beaverbrook. Lord Beaverbrook.' 'Not at all', said the doctor. 'You told me it was Lord Willoughby de Broke.'

By this time Lord Beaverbrook was on his way to America, as the party had been given on the eve of his departure. The newspapers in England never mentioned the event. The American Pressmen were either more active, or less discreet than Fleet Street. Beaverbrook was greeted in New York with large posters carrying the news, 'Lord Beaverbrook Gives a Party'.

On his journey seeking the sun in the South of France, the West Indies, and elsewhere, Beaverbrook kept touch with his men by telephone and also by Dictaphone. From the four corners of the world the tapes arrived. Curt messages of honey or vitriol, stick or carrot, goad or curb flew in according to the views of the Old Master.

Once I had written an article on some of the well-known politicians of the day. I ended by speaking of a lady prominent in public affairs who had forgotten to give the facts about her age in *Who's Who*. Rudely, boldly, I guessed the missing number. A few days later a tape arrived from some far place. I was bidden by Lord Beaverbrook's secretary to come and hear the Master's Voice. It ran something as follows, 'Now, Peter, that article you sent me. Baldwin—too long, too long, too long. Lloyd George—too long, too long, too long. Churchill—

too long, too long, too long.' Then the voice rose in tone nearly an octave. It bubbled with glee and malice. It said, 'And the lady you mention, Peter. Too young, too young, too young.'

I was younger then. But I shall never be too old to enjoy the zest and zing of his attack on life or on those who lived around him.

3

FAITHS AND FAMILY

Beaverbrook the Idealist

BEAVERBROOK could say with Alan Breck, 'Am I no' a bonnie fechter?' And his story is the opposite of John Paul's verse:

> I care not a pin what the world may say
> In regard to the wrong and right;
> My money goes as well as my song
> For the dog that keeps out of the fight.

Beaverbrook was a battler all his days. If there were no battle to join in, he was apt to make one.

Churchill used to say privately to those who could inform him, 'Tell me, which way is the little man going? I'm off in the opposite direction.' He meant, of course, Lloyd George.

And that was too often the position of Beaverbrook himself in terms of public opinion. 'Tell me,' he seemed to ask, 'which way is public opinion going? I'm off in the opposite direction.' It was a joy in antagonism, a love of being hated, a disregard of popular outlook, a satisfaction in being odd man out. It was a form of pride of spirit that was a weakness in the man. And from time to time it meant that his delight in defiance warped his influence and wasted his toil.

One great theme of his fighting life was his loyalty to the idea of Empire. He was more consistent to this vision than any other man in the world. Another theme was his faith in God.

Critics may sneer that his actions belied such faith. Most honest men, however faithful, can say the same of themselves. And any who doubt the reality of that faith will misunderstand the man.

His faith in God and his vision of Empire began in his youth. His father came from Scotland to Canada in 1864. Beaverbrook, then Max Aitken, was born in Ontario, but when he was eleven months old, his father was called as Presbyterian Minister from Ontario to Newcastle, New Brunswick. The father was at that time forty-six years old. He had five children of whom Max was the youngest. Five more were born in New Brunswick, one of them dying in infancy.

The whole family lived on an income of fifteen hundred dollars a year. Beaverbrook gave his son Max, and his daughter Janet, gifts of more than a million pounds each.

Max is a newspaperman like his father. And a first-rate newspaperman too. He is Chairman of the Board of the Beaverbrook Newspapers. His delight is sailing. He owns a yacht. In spite of that, he has multiplied his father's gift with prudence. The trees and young forests around Cherkley, which for over fifty years was Lord Beaverbrook's Surrey home, are a tribute to the foresight of the son Max.

Janet, the daughter, also interests herself in the land. She has eighty cows. But nowadays some cows do not yield as much cash as cream. You have to pour gold coins into the milk-churns each morning. She has seven mares and fifteen colts. And while her brother, Max, rides the waves, she and her family are astride the saddle. She owns a house in Barbados, and each winter goes there with her household.

Both son and daughter live higher than their father. And he sat in a chair grinning with glee as he said, 'We've come a long way from the Reverend William Aitken, my father, who lived with the whole family on fifteen hundred dollars a year, haven't we?' In childhood days Max spent much time in the woods alone. He was the rebel of the family. He refused to sit in the pew of privilege reserved in church for the family of the manse. He used to sit in the gallery staring down as his father preached the gospel, with his long white beard, flowing gown, and black gloves.

In childhood Max Aitken made a friendship which was to last for life and play its part in history. It was with Richard Bedford Bennett, Viscount Bennett of Mickleham, one-time Prime Minister of Canada. The two first met in 1889 when Bennett was a schoolmaster at Douglastown and Max Aitken was a schoolboy at Newcastle. Bennett was nineteen, Aitken ten at the time. Douglastown and Newcastle are on the Miramichi River. Aitken travelled from Douglastown to Newcastle, a journey of four or five miles, by boat with Bennett. Aitken was everything that Bennett was not. Aitken was full of mischief, fun, and bedevilment. Bennett carried a Bible about with him. He disliked swearing. Gambling and dancing he deplored. He was against smoking and against drinking.

Maybe the uprightness of his new friend challenged the combative instinct of the young son of the Presbyterian manse.

In life it is true that the biggest propagandists are people who drink, smoke, swear, and gamble. They never can rest till they have everyone around them doing the same. At the same time, they protest with passion their love of liberty. Be that as it may, in the early days of their friendship Aitken used to stimulate Bennett by discussions on doctrinal questions. Bennett was a militant Methodist. Aitken used to taunt him with expositions of the Presbyterian doctrine of predestination. He would quote the following poem to Bennett:

> I know that God is wroth with me
> For I was born in sin.
> My heart is so exceeding vile
> Damnation dwells therein.

Awake I sin, asleep I sin,
I sin with every breath.
When Adam fell he went to hell
And damned us all to death.

This poem would arouse Bennett to a rage. He was a man who all through life until the very evening of his days had a strong temper, and in his youth found it hard to control.

In 1895 Bennett ran his first political race as candidate for Alderman, in the newly created town of Chatham, New Brunswick. On 12 June 1941 Bennett, who had just been made a Viscount in the British House of Lords, wrote to Max, his old friend, saying, 'Forty-five years ago I was a candidate for the office of Alderman. Senator Snowball was a candidate for the Mayoralty opposed by Dr. Joseph Benson. I was supported by a youth of some seventeen years who, with his bicycle, hurried many to the polls and was a factor, a real factor, in my election.' Bennett won by one vote. And he ends the letter, 'So you had a very real part in my first successful venture into public life'.

Not long after this first adventure at the polls, the two young men quarrelled. Bennett had gone West to the Alberta Bar. Aitken followed him. At first all went well, and Bennett, who was lonely, welcomed his friend. He was at this time eating immense meals as he believed that if he put on weight he would be more impressive. He used to eat a plate of porridge, bacon, and many eggs, quantities of toast, honey, and marmalade for breakfast. Lunch and dinner were on the same scale. Aitken was less fond of the food, but of course did not share Bennett's views on teetotalism. Bennett became impatient with Aitken's attitudes to life. He used to say to him, 'If only your character equalled your ability'.

Aitken borrowed 250 dollars from a bank and bought with it a bowling alley. Business opened daily at 6 p.m. Aitken's partner took in the money from 6 to 8, while Aitken set up the pins. After 8 o'clock duties were reversed. Aitken would play the clients and if the client won he got his game free. If he lost he paid. Bennett was so angry with these activities that he broke off all communications with Aitken. He would not speak to him. Nevertheless, Aitken and his partner paid off the 250 dollars to the bank, exchanged the bowling alley for a stationery and tobacco store, and sold this store for a profit.

Bennett now wanted to run for the North-West Legislature. He made up the quarrel. He asked Aitken to help him. Aitken did so and Bennett won the day.

It was at this time, the start of the twentieth century, that both Bennett and Aitken were captured by Joseph Chamberlain's vision of Empire. As it coloured the political outlook of Beaverbrook to the end of his life, it is important to understand it.

Joseph Chamberlain was a rebel. As a Radical manufacturer in Birmingham, he led the campaign which in 1870 established primary education. He enraged those with gold in their purses and blue in their veins. He hoped to succeed Gladstone as leader of the Liberals, but Gladstone refused to die and instead adopted the policy of Irish Home Rule. So Chamberlain broke with him.

Lord Salisbury, as Conservative Prime Minister, in 1895 offered him the Exchequer or the War Office. Instead, Chamberlain chose the Colonial Office.

Halévy (*History of the English People in the Nineteenth Century*, Volume V) says of him, 'If there was ever a man to enlarge the scope of his commission, that man was Chamberlain whose ambition was the more insatiable because it had been so long unsatisfied and who had reached the age of sixty when at last he found himself in a position to play the part in his country's history of which he felt himself capable. Everyone in England or on the continent knew that pallid face, those pursed lips, that faultless frock-coat, that orchid in the buttonhole, and that eloquence at once cold and vehement which infuriated his opponents. By nature a firebrand, his words and actions alike kindled a conflagration.'

Salisbury checked Chamberlain. Salisbury was older, successful, established. Chamberlain wanted to thrust forward and achieve in his last years of active life the triumphs that had for long escaped him. He would risk anything, even war, to achieve his aims. In one speech he said, 'War is no doubt a horrible thing, but even war itself would be cheaply purchased if in a great and noble cause the Stars and Stripes and the Union Jack should wave together over an Anglo-Saxon alliance'.

In October 1902 Chamberlain visited South Africa after the end of the Boer War, and on his return on 15 March 1902 he made a speech which shook the country. He frankly stated that Britain should abandon free trade as a policy and should immediately work for Empire free trade, which would mean tariffs on non-Empire goods.

The force of Chamberlain's conviction swept aside the inertia of the old Houses of Cecil and Derby. Chamberlain did not suffer from the snobbery towards the Colonies and towards America which scourged some sections of British life. In the words of Halévy, 'Chamberlain was entirely devoid of the prejudice against the Americans usual among the Tories'.

For years most of the British public backed the practical idea of Empire which Chamberlain put forward, even if the details of the dream never were fully realized.

It was this idea which interested young Bennett and young Aitken. They were struck too by the knowledge of countless, nameless men, in deep colds and torrid heats of an Empire which stretched from Arctic to Antarctic, often for small human rewards, sweating, suffering, instructing for a life-time, sometimes leaving their very bones to rot in alien soil or seas, for the sake of an imperishable glory that was Britain.

Nor must it be forgotten that the early ideals of Joseph Chamberlain helped to cultivate the seeds of the Anglo-American alliance that has proved a winning combination in two world wars. Looking further ahead from the turn of the century, those who nowadays shrug at the concept of Empire should remember this. In World War II, France on the one side, Italy on the other, laid down their arms. America and Russia joined in the conflict when, but not until, they were attacked. Yet from the start of the conflict, self-governing Dominions, like Canada, Australia, New Zealand, yes, South Africa too, chose to hazard their blood and treasure at the side of the Mother country.

And the Ottawa Agreements for a measure of Imperial Preference in 1932, while not all that Beaverbrook asked for, were the outcome of his own agitation against the Tory leadership of the time (so like Joseph Chamberlain's battles against the earlier Lord Salisbury). It produced the only real revival in trade between two world wars.

But all this tale of triumph and tragedy, of opportunities half-understood and half-grasped by half-hearted politicians in Britain, Canada, and elsewhere, was lost in the future to young Aitken and Bennett as they talked together in those far-off days.

On New Year's Day, 1904, in Halifax, Nova Scotia, Bennett, staying at Aitken's flat, talked all through the day about an Empire policy. He proposed to Aitken that one day both men should sit in the British House of Commons with the British Empire as their 'pillar of cloud by day and pillar of fire by night'.

In October 1906 Aitken wrote to Bennett predicting that his friend would become the Prime Minister of Canada. He declared, 'I have no doubt of the ultimate place you will take'. It is interesting to record that when Bonar Law became Prime Minister of Great Britain on 23 October 1922, Bennett wrote Aitken in the following terms, 'More than ten years ago I dined one Sunday evening with Mr. Bonar Law, Miss Law and yourself at Pembroke Lodge. I remember your remarks as we came away and still later your observations as to the likelihood of Bonar becoming Prime Minister.'

So it is true to say that Aitken picked his two friends Bennett and Bonar Law as Prime Ministers of their countries many years before they won that race.

By 1910 Aitken had made a fortune. He made it by many business hazards, including an enterprise in cement which was in effect a take-over bid of the Canadian cement industry, financed by bankers who trusted him. He moved to England. He tried to launch himself into the political arena in support of the Chamberlain Empire Policy. And suddenly, by a fling of fortune's dice, he found himself in the British Parliament. On 15 November 1910 he was at Bonar Law's house in London. Bonar Law was a fellow Canadian, and also a son of the manse. He had become a friend of Aitken. A deputation arrived from Ashton-under-Lyne seeking a Tory candidate. Bonar Law refused the offer, but mentioned Aitken's name. Aitken was astonished to find that by 2 December 1910 he was the Member of Parliament for the Lancashire constituency. At that time he received from Bennett in Canada in a letter a statement of his Empire faith, 'I believe that Canada awaits the coming of a man with a vision, a statesman (R. B. Bennett) with a revelation, one who sees our destiny and who will arouse the latent patriotism and pride of our race and by appealing to all that is best within us, lead us to an Imperial federation where among the nations that comprise the union, Canada must take a foremost place and in time direct the large destinies of our world-wide empire'.

Bonar Law was twenty-one years older than Aitken. In 1910 Aitken was thirty-one, Law fifty-two. Law was unlike Aitken in many of his ways. He never drank but puffed at a pipe without ceasing. He did not care about food, scarcely noticing what was put before him. He gulped vegetables, rice pudding, and milk with rapidity.

His hobbies were chess and bridge. For preference he read only the newspapers, and light novels.

Within a year of Aitken entering Parliament, the then leader of the Tory opposition, bachelor Arthur James Balfour, resigned. He had led his party three times to electoral defeat. A B.M.G. (Balfour Must Go) tide had begun to flow through the clubs and week-end parties, where, in those days, so many political issues were decided. Balfour yielded, saying, in the characteristic way of the man who later Clemenceau called at the Peace Conference of 1919 '*cette vieille fille*', 'I am tired'. Two candidates were put forward to succeed him.

One was Walter Long, supported by county Squires. The other Austen Chamberlain, supported by city Gentry. In spite of being Joseph Chamberlain's elder son, Austen said with truth, 'Tariff Reform is the millstone round my neck'.

Aitken saw a chance in the division among the Tories. He persuaded his friend, Bonar Law, to let it be known that he would be a candidate for the Tory leadership. When Long's men seemed in the lead, Law's supporters backed Chamberlain. When Chamberlain led, Law's supporters, incited by Aitken, backed Long. It soon became clear that Bonar Law was the only man who could be elected to Tory leadership without splitting the party. On 13 November 1911, five days after Balfour resigned, Long's and Chamberlain's supporters united to elect Law leader of the Party. Walter Long proposed his election. Austen Chamberlain seconded it.

Lloyd George, when he heard of it, said, 'The Tories have stumbled on their very best man. He is a very clever fellow. I like him.'

Bonar Law said of Lloyd George about the same time, 'I like Lloyd George. He is a very nice man. But he is the most dangerous little man that ever lived.'

The two Canadians had triumphed over the Tory establishment. Their struggle struck a chord of response in the heart of Lloyd George, another 'aginner'.

Aitken–George–Law—it was a combination of character, courage, and cunning that was destined to remould the shape of British politics in the tempest of the years that lay ahead.

Here let something be said about Beaverbrook's personal loyalties. He always showed too strong an adherence in public life to those who were his private friends.

When a man makes boast that he puts personal affection first, then his judgement on public affairs may suffer. Beaverbrook was sometimes unseasonable and unreasonable in his support of Bonar Law. The man could do no wrong in the eyes of his friend. But Bonar Law—and Britain—suffered from this blind adherence.

E. M. Forster has said, 'If I had to choose between betraying my country and betraying my friend, I hope I would have the guts to betray my country'. Beaverbrook would never have echoed such a view. He would not betray his country. But Max's over-allegiance to friendship may sometimes have made him miss the maximum in his attitudes to Britain.

During World War II, I have been told that Lord Beaverbrook would never lift up his voice against Churchill in Cabinet. No matter how deeply he felt a cleavage of viewpoint, no matter how strong his forebodings about the course that was advocated, his lips were sealed in Cabinet except in Churchill's support.

It was for a different reason that another of Churchill's colleagues bowed to the telephone when the war-time Prime Minister was on the line. There was no timidity or fawning in Beaverbrook's attitude to Churchill. Indeed, in private he would argue and plead to shift plans and to win his way. But his fellow Ministers knew that in Beaverbrook Churchill had a friend who would sustain him, right or wrong, in Cabinet council. The unthinking may see virtue in this attitude. But men with a larger responsibility and understanding of life's ways will perceive there a flaw both weak and perilous.

4

DESTINY & DISAPPOINTMENT

Beaverbrook the Politician

No man foresaw the outcome when German boots went clumping across the Belgian border on 4 August 1914. People hoped for victory or feared defeat. They did not comprehend that a convulsion had begun that would change the shape of civilization.

Wrenches and rumbles of that cataclysm still send a shudder round this planet. That event, the first World War between mighty states that in those days still thought of themselves as Christian, brought death to ancient kingdoms as well as to millions of homes, both humble and great. It brought to birth and maturity new ideas of how man should be governed which affect all humanity. The end of it is not yet.

And the political life of Britain was changed. The war which this country might have lost, was won. The Liberal Party, for nearly a century a powerful element in our affairs, was finished as a force for nearly fifty years. The Labour Party became an alternative Government to the Conservatives. And for the first time in British history, a man of the people, an unpolished, ungentlemanly rebel, a man who never 'played the game', but often won it, became war-winning Premier of the land.

His name was David Lloyd George.

In these affairs Max Aitken played no small a part. Without Bonar Law, Lloyd George could never have become Prime Minister. Without Max Aitken, Bonar Law would never have carried Lloyd George to triumph on his back.

When the war began, the Rt. Hon. Henry Herbert Asquith was Prime Minister as head of a Liberal Government. He seemed indestructible. He was friend of the King. (When Asquith fell, the King (George V) wrote in his diary, 'It will cause a panic in the City and in America and do harm to the allies. It is a great blow to me and will, I fear, buck up the Germans.') Asquith, by his second marriage (to Margot Tennant, daughter of Sir Charles Tennant), had built links with Society, which in those days still held much power in the land. He had won his way by brains and brilliance to a scholarship, then a Fellowship at Balliol College, Oxford, and a commanding prominence in Parliament. He was an intellectual giant, but with a heart often given to soft drawing-room lights and smart personalities rather than enmeshed in the sweat and struggle and sorrows of humanity.

The first Government crisis of the First World War came in 1915. Asquith asked for the resignations of all his Liberal Cabinet colleagues and then took Conservatives, including Bonar Law, into the Government with him. The first Coalition was formed. It happened because of a row between Lord Fisher, the First Sea Lord, and Mr. Winston Churchill (at that time a Liberal), First Lord of the Admiralty.

Jackie Fisher, the old tarry Admiral, had removed the needless spit and polish from the British Fleet near the start of the century, and made those grey, lean ships one of the deadliest instruments of war in modern history.

Churchill had boldly mobilized that Fleet when some wavered and others wished to waste more time as the war loomed on. Churchill dreamed of turning the flank of Britain's enemies with her naval power and forcing a swift and final victory through the Dardanelles. Fisher sarcastically described such schemes as 'subsidiary operations'.

News came that the British battleship *Goliath* had been torpedoed in the Aegean Sea by a Turkish destroyer. More than five hundred British seamen died.

Fisher decided to quit. Meeting Lloyd George, then Liberal Chancellor of the Exchequer, he baldly announced, 'I've resigned'. This was the first news anyone had of the Admiral's intention to abandon his post at the pitch of a deadly war.

The Home Secretary (McKenna), a friend of both Fisher and Churchill, tried to make peace between the two men. He went knocking at Fisher's door at the Admiralty. There was no reply. But the Home Secretary spied Fisher peeping at him through drawn blinds, and continued to bombard the door with his knuckles until it was opened. Despite efforts since that time to prove that this reconstruction of the Government was caused by something other than Fisher's retreat, this is not so. When Fisher quit, reconstruction became inevitable.

When Fisher pulled down the blinds at the Admiralty and peeked at McKenna through the chinks, he was in effect saying, 'Go away. I'm not here. And I'm not going to be here.'

Finally he let McKenna in. But he would not budge. Instead he took the night train to Scotland and laid his bones to rest as guest of the Duchess of Hamilton. (The ghost of Lord Nelson, another great sailor and servant of England who used to seek solace with another Lady Hamilton, must have suffered pangs in Paradise at this denial by Jackie Fisher of Nelson's everlasting wartime challenge, 'England expects every man to do his duty'.)

Jackie Fisher sent Bonar Law, then leader of the Tory Opposition in Parliament, an envelope with a newspaper cutting which said, 'Lord Fisher was received in audience of the King and remained there about half an hour'. This communication was anonymous. But Law had no difficulty in recognising Fisher's scrawl on the envelope.

Law told Lloyd George he would be forced to raise the question of Fisher's resignation in Parliament. The Tories at this time hated Churchill more than almost any other Liberal. They welcomed the chance of attacking him in his position as First Lord of the Admiralty. Lloyd George at once said, 'That means coalition'. He and Bonar Law went to see Asquith. The first Coalition was born, with Asquith remaining as Prime Minister.

Churchill, to the delight of the Tories, was demoted from the Admiralty and given the Chancellorship of the Duchy of Lancaster. He resigned from the Government when the Dardanelles Expedition was withdrawn. The Coalition was not satisfactory to the Tories. For Asquith gave his Liberals the plum posts, while Bonar Law and his Tories had to put up with the pips and peel, the lesser responsibilities.

The war was not going well for Britain. There was slackness at home. Men talked of Peace by Negotiation. And the direction of the fighting forces seemed lax. It was in control of Kitchener, an almost legendary figure in his own lifetime, a hero of the nation, Asquith's Secretary of State for War.

Kitchener was an odd and interesting character. He was full of quirks and foibles. He refused to appoint a Presbyterian as chief of the chaplains in the army, though the man's talents and seniority entitled him to the job. 'No fancy religions', said Kitchener. Lloyd George and Bonar Law, both nonconformists, tackled him. With reluctance he gave way.

When Bonar Law, as Colonial Secretary and responsible for the former German West African colonies, told Kitchener, 'I propose to appoint General Smuts to command in German West Africa', Kitchener replied, 'My *generals* would not be prepared to serve under *Mister* Smuts'. It was Smuts, of course, who had fought against Kitchener's generals in the battles of the Boer War. They did not call him *Mister* Smuts in those days. Nor when he handed in his acceptance of the terms of peace at the end of that war, and a nation waited on tiptoe the outcome of his decision.

Kitchener loved secrecy. He said, 'I do not tell the Cabinet my secrets. If I do, they go home and tell their wives. All except —— who goes and tells other men's wives.' Kitchener was himself unmarried.

Lloyd George, who had moved from the Exchequer to the

Ministry of Munitions when Asquith first formed his Coalition, was strongly critical of Kitchener. Kitchener was sent to Russia. His mission was to encourage our Allies and see what more could be done to hold up their arms in battle.

It is possible, even probable, that Asquith contemplated removing him from his post as Secretary of State for War. But this has never been disclosed.

Kitchener sailed into the night. There was an explosion, whether from mine or torpedo has never been surely known. Down went the ship into the cold, dark depths of ocean, and carried Kitchener, hero of many a land battle, to the sand, ooze, and water of his tomb.

Asquith distrusted Lloyd George. He feared him as possible rival in leadership of the Liberal Party. He planned to give Kitchener's place at the War Office, with its dynamic power so directly bearing upon events, to anyone rather than Lloyd George.

Lloyd George met Bonar Law at lunch with Max Aitken at Cherkley. Lloyd George said to Bonar Law, 'These other men are not going to have the War Office. It's too dangerous. Either you have it—or I do.' 'Well,' answered Bonar Law, 'you have it.'

Law genuinely thought Lloyd George the better man. It was a restraint and diffidence which his friend Max Aitken found hard to swallow. In any event, Bonar Law agreed to back Lloyd George's claim to the War Office, if necessary with the threat of resignation.

He telephoned to Asquith and was told that if he wanted to see him, he would have to motor to Berkshire, fifty miles away. This irritated him. It was too late to go that evening. He was due to leave for France next day.

As soon as Asquith heard the purpose of the visit, he offered the War Office to Bonar Law. Law declined. He overbore Asquith's objections to Lloyd George, who got the job. It was not an appointment Asquith wanted to make. It was one he had to make.

Aitken at once drove Law to Dover on his way to Paris to see some of the French Ministers.

Now the C.I.G.S. crowd, the military big-wigs, did not want either Law or George at the War Office. But of the two they preferred Law. They looked with horror on the prospect of Lloyd George going there. They knew there would be a row. And there was. Aitken had arranged to telegraph Bob Whigham (General Sir Robert Whigham, then Deputy Chief of the Army Council) which man was to be the new War Minister. The code arranged was 'Alpha' for Law, 'Omega' for George. Aitken telegraphed 'Omega'. The reply came, 'My God'.

Aitken pondered these events. He had the quality of recognizing political dynamite and knowing how to use it. He said to himself, 'Asquith has been beaten. If you can beat a man once, you can beat him twice.' The legend of the Prime Minister's invulnerability had been destroyed.

Some months later there was a week-end party at Cherkley. Bonar Law was there. So was Churchill, out of office and in the flood of frustration that comes to those who feel able to serve their country in high places and rough times but are prevented by events from doing so. Churchill assailed Bonar Law in golden English about the sins of the Government. Bonar Law was enraged by Churchill. He thought that all Churchill wanted was a job for himself.

Max Aitken tried to stop Churchill who he could see was angering Bonar Law. But Churchill's oratory flowed on. At last Law dammed the flood. He said, 'Very well. If that is the way you feel about the Government, we'll have an election and see what the country feels about it.'

It was at that moment that the perils of this threat struck Aitken. He saw that at a wartime General Election Asquith's Liberals would be unopposed. Law, as Tory Leader and loyal to Asquith, the Liberal Prime Minister, would see to this. All the Tories who were critics of the Government would be opposed and defeated by Tories friendly to Law and supported by Asquith's Liberals.

The Tory Party would be split asunder. Bonar Law would be a maimed man in public life. Asquith would be the unchallenged ruler of the country.

Aitken's resolve to help organize political revolution, which ended in the overthrow of Asquith and the establishment of Lloyd George and Bonar Law as the war-winners, was born. His motives may be summarized as follows:

1. A determination to preserve the position of his friend Bonar Law. Through that friendship he had best hope one day of getting his Empire policies accepted by the country.

2. A resolve to maintain the unity of the Tory Party.

3. A purpose to pursue the war to a victorious ending and to prevent any movement towards Peace by Negotiation.

By the evening of 6 December 1916 Asquith had been destroyed and Lloyd George became Prime Minister of Britain. Accounts of the intrigues and risks, bluffs and frailties, courage and cravenness that brought this to pass have often been given. It is for my purposes enough to pick out one or two incidents from the multitude of those events.

Bonar Law had the chance at that time of being Prime Minister. Aitken believed he had earned it. But Bonar Law pushed Lloyd George into the job, genuinely believing he was the better man to win the war.

At the time, and later, many believed Lloyd George had played his part in overthrowing Asquith simply to take his place himself. But Lloyd George at first refused to become Prime Minister. Beaverbrook, in his own account of those events (*Politicians and the War, 1914–1916*, pp. 485, 486), writes as follows: 'Those who worked on the "personal ambition" theory of Lloyd George's activities would have expected him to jump eagerly to seize on the offer [of becoming Premier]. As a matter of fact, Lloyd George did exactly the opposite. "No," he said in effect, "I don't want to be Premier.

I have not been fighting for the Premiership, but simply to get rid of the Asquith incubus. Give me the Chairmanship of the War Council and (turning to Bonar Law) I am perfectly content and would prefer to serve under you." It will be no use saying this as a matter of hearsay or second-hand gossip. It was in my presence that Lloyd George told Bonar Law with the most transparent sincerity that he thought Bonar Law's Premiership would be the wisest solution and that he wished to serve under him.'

In the event, Lloyd George took top place and Bonar Law served at his side till victory and beyond it. Of Max Aitken's influence on Bonar Law, let Lloyd George speak:[1] 'He [Bonar Law] possessed real courage. It was not the blind dare of the reckless or the buoyant courage of the sanguine. He anticipated trouble everywhere and mostly exaggerated it. Nevertheless he faced it without faltering if it came. He was both fearless and apprehensive. His great phrase in beginning and often in ending an interview was, "*There is lots of trouble ahead*". Any manœuvring in the House of Commons, especially among the supporters of the Government, worried him. On these occasions, when he was more miserable than usual, I used to say to him, "Let us swop jobs. You can take mine and I will run yours." That generally put an end to the discussion. He shrank from accepting the supreme responsibility for decisions which might be right but which would, if they turned out to be wrong, entail irreparable injury to the interests of the country. During these years, almost every day decisions of that fatefulness had to be taken. A reluctance to decide when there was a serious difference of opinion was a curious defect in so resolute and truly brave a man. But there it undoubtedly was. It was probably due to an inherent diffidence which caused him to distrust his own judgement, coupled with a strong blend of conscientiousness and caution which made him fearful of doing

[1] *War Memoirs of David Lloyd George*, Volume II, pp. 1027, 1028.

the wrong thing. His attachment to Lord Beaverbrook was largely, though by no means entirely, attributable to this natural defect. He found a support and a strength in this resolute friend whose practical shrewdness gave him confidence and whose personal devotion he knew to be beyond challenge and question. He thus came to rely upon him in every emergency of his public and private life. His remarkable success in so short a time and in a party so constituted as the Tory Party was undoubtedly due to Beaverbrook's prompting and management. Mr. Bonar Law was not without ambition, but this motive was not strong enough to overcome the hesitancies of so anxious a temperament. Mr. Asquith once said of him that he was "meekly ambitious". Lord Beaverbrook's forceful insistence and unfailing backing cured all that. He shoved him almost brutally to the front. He firmly believed him to be the best man to succeed Mr. Balfour when the latter was driven out of the leadership of the Conservative Party. I was certainly of the same opinion at the time, and I had no reason to change my view afterwards.'

Beaverbrook, asked about these views of Lloyd George, replied, 'I do not agree with his assessment. It is true that when Bonar Law and Lloyd George planned to displace Asquith in 1916, Bonar Law was ill. He may have relied on me more than before. But if you look beneath the surface, our relationship was different.'

Here is how Sir Austen Chamberlain in his book *Down the Years* sees the relationship: 'It is characteristic of Lord Beaverbrook's whole attitude to Bonar Law to represent himself merely as the clarifying medium which enabled Bonar Law to precipitate his own thoughts and perceive them clearly. No one who ever saw them together can accept that account of their relationship.'

A revealing remark is that made by Beaverbrook to Bonar Law after Law had won a struggle for leadership: 'Remember, you are a great man now.'

Bonar Law replied, 'If I am a great man, then all great men are frauds'. Most men have enough common sense to question in their own hearts their own 'greatness'. But it is interesting that Beaverbrook, a man of sensitivity coupled with a cynical but almost complete understanding of the weaknesses of human nature, found it useful to say such a thing to Law at a moment of triumph.

Churchill was not given any job in the Lloyd George administration which followed Asquith. Few trusted Churchill at that time. Lloyd George asked Bonar Law, 'Is Churchill more dangerous when he is *for* you than when he is *against* you?' Bonar Law replied, 'I would rather have him against us every time'.

(In a letter to a friend on 14 October 1914 Bonar Law had written of Churchill, 'He has very unusual intellectual ability, but at the same time, he seems to have an entirely unbalanced mind which is a real danger at a time like this'.)

After Lloyd George became Prime Minister, Bonar Law, joking with him, said, 'George,' (this was how Bonar Law always addressed him) 'you know Winston means to seize your Liberal leadership'. (Churchill was a Liberal at the time.) 'Maybe,' answered Lloyd George, 'but he will get your leadership of the Conservative Party first.' In this, George was a better prophet than Law. Churchill never led the Liberals, but was elected as Leader of the Conservative Party when he carried Britain to victory in World War II.

Bonar Law lent Lloyd George the moral mantle he needed. A most discerning view of the two men was given by Philip Snowden, Labour's Iron Chancellor, who began life preaching social revolution in the Yorkshire vales and villages and ended it amid the ermine and purple of the House of Lords. Snowden was a friend of Max Beaverbrook. The men would dine together and sometimes they would sing. 'Ilkla Moor' and 'The Red Flag' were among their best performances.

Snowden used to pronounce the word 'bloody' as if it

rhymed with the word 'broody'. He said of Bonar Law and Lloyd George, 'Bonar Law comes down to the House of Commons and tells bloody lies. We all believe it. Lloyd George comes down there and tells us the naked truth. We all shout "bloody liar".'

Lloyd George put it in another way. He said to Stanley Baldwin, later Lord Baldwin, 'That's the difference between Bonar Law and me. Poor Bonar can't bear being called a liar. Now I don't mind a bit.' And Baldwin himself, describing years later Bonar Law's victory in the 1922 election which enabled him to succeed Lloyd George as Premier of Britain, said at an Oxford dinner, 'One morning people opened their newspapers and read that Lloyd George had said of Bonar Law that he was "honest to the verge of simplicity". And they said, "By God, that's what we are looking for". So they made Bonar Law Prime Minister.'

It is an irony of history that in 1916, Aitken, having played a master role in the destruction of Asquith, destroyed himself as well. It happened in this way.

When the battle was won and Asquith, who a few days before seemed a political Goliath, had been tumbled over, Aitken walked with David under the trees of Cherkley. That David was of course David Lloyd George. As the two men walked under the trees, Lloyd George in clear and precise terms promised Aitken that he would be in charge of the Board of Trade in the new Government which was being formed. The Board of Trade was an office much coveted by Aitken. In wartime it was the department responsible for movement of troops. That was a task which Aitken felt able by his training to perform and where he believed he could serve this country well. Also he saw clearly the political future which it could open up.

Aitken left Lloyd George by the ancient yew-trees. He went at once to Bonar Law for he felt under an obligation to him and did not want to accept the Board of Trade without his friend's consent. Bonar Law listened. He made no comment. Aitken felt free to accept Lloyd George's offer, and he did so.

In those days, there was a rule that any Member of Parliament who accepted an office of profit under the Crown had to resign from his seat and seek re-election. A Cabinet post, such as the Board of Trade, was an office of profit under the Crown. So Aitken's wife went north to Ashton-under-Lyne, the constituency which Aitken represented, to prepare his friends for the coming election. She made a public speech saying her husband was about to take office under the Crown and telling them they needed to prepare for a by-election.

Meanwhile, in the south strong men were objecting to Aitken's appointment. The first objection came from Lord Derby. Then Cecil, Chamberlain, Curzon, and Long, the most powerful Conservative figures of the day apart from Bonar Law, all objected. They resented Aitken, not because of his failure but because of his success. He had challenged the Establishment. In the face of their objections to Lloyd George, and support of Asquith, this young Canadian had defied them. They had lost. He had won. They were ready to serve themselves under the new Prime Minister, but fear and jealousy played a part in their resolve to down Aitken. Also Aitken had made his own fortune. He had a Canadian accent and he had a mind of originality. These were three formidable disadvantages, in those days, for a man who was about to enter the Cabinet.

Lloyd George quailed. The man who held a nation steady before the massed might of her enemies trembled before the political pressure of his Conservative allies. He ran out on his offer to Aitken. But he did not tell Aitken that he had run out. It was a Friday. Aitken spent the whole of that day waiting for a call from Lloyd George. None came. In the days and weeks beforehand the telephone-bell had been ringing day and night, night and day. Now it was silent. Aitken had fallen from a state of extreme activity to one of complete idleness, weariness, and misery. The man who had been at the heart of great events found himself out of things. He thought of sending word to his wife to stop what she was doing in the north. But he did not know whether tomorrow or next day he might be plunged into the by-election battle there. He could not stop. He could not go on. He did not know what to do.

At last he left his hotel and went down to the War Office. Inside the War Office he knew that Lloyd George was building the new Cabinet. He had intended to go in and ask what was happening. But when he reached the War Office he felt he could not go inside and seem to be cadging for the job. So he walked around in the darkness.

There by chance he met Sir Reginald Brade, then Permanent Under-Secretary at the War Office. Brade, coming out of the War Office, told him that jobs had already been settled in many cases and that the Board of Trade was going to Albert Stanley (later Lord Ashfield).

Aitken went home utterly distressed. He telephoned his wife. He said to her, 'Come back. I can't talk over the phone. I'll explain everything to you when you get here.'

Next day Lloyd George telephoned. He asked himself to lunch and brought Bonar Law with him. Aitken was savage. Lloyd George said to him, 'You're a tiger, but a good tiger'. Aitken replied, 'Not so good'. Lloyd George left, but later sent a letter asking Aitken to go to the House of Lords to answer for the business departments in that assembly. Aitken did not know what to do. He went down to Cherkley.

Lord Birkenhead (he was then F. E. Smith) followed him. He stayed the Saturday and Sunday there. He had one of the sharpest swords and keenest minds in British public life. He said to Aitken, 'The only way out for you is a peerage. Take it.' So Aitken wrote accepting the peerage.

On the Sunday, Bonar Law arrived at Cherkley. He said, 'You've ridden too high. There's such a row going on that you will have to refuse the peerage.'

Aitken sat down and wrote to Lloyd George refusing the peerage. His cup was filled with bitterness. He had believed that in view of what Lloyd George owed to him and of all that he had done, George would have been ready to ride the storm of opposition. His wife's journey to Ashton-under-Lyne was public property. He was in a dreadful dilemma.

On the Monday, Bonar Law asked Aitken to go and see him. Aitken went to his office. His friend said, 'You must at once accept the peerage. We need your seat in Parliament at Ashton-under-Lyne for Stanley.' The truth was they had promised Max Aitken's seat in Parliament to Albert Stanley, the man who had been given the seat in the Cabinet which Lloyd George had promised Aitken. Aitken was doubly dispossessed. On Bonar Law's advice, he handed over his seat in the House of Commons to Stanley. Thinking it was the only way out of his dilemma, he joined the House of Lords. He regretted it ever after, to the end of his life.

Lord Derby might have saved Aitken from this disaster of ennoblement. He opposed Aitken's peerage saying that if another peerage was to be given, it should go to some other Lancashire Member of Parliament, not to Aitken. But, unhappily for Aitken, Derby was defeated—and Aitken became Lord Beaverbrook.

Another man who might have saved him from his fate was King George V. He said to his friends that Asquith had been 'tumbled by intrigue'. He was angry because he had not been consulted before Aitken was invited to accept the peerage. Further he did not see what public service Aitken had rendered which entitled him to this promotion in 1916. However, the King gave way.

It was Beaverbrook himself who first disclosed the King's resistance to the peerage. Later Sir Harold Nicolson took up the tale in his book *King George V* (pages 511, 512):

'Far more complicated and distressing were the constant difficulties that arose over the bestowal of political honours.

Ministers were inclined to make promises to individuals before His Majesty's pleasure had been obtained. A flagrant case of such disregard occurred in 1916. Mr. Lloyd George and Mr. Bonar Law, desiring to obtain a seat in the House of Commons for one of the new Ministers, offered a peerage to a Conservative Member representing a safe constituency. The King, when asked for his consent, replied that he did not "see his way" to approve of this honour since he did not consider that the "public services" of the individual in question "called for such special recognition". Mr. Lloyd George replied that any refusal would "place him in a position of great embarrassment" and begged Lord Stamfordham to discuss the matter with Mr. Bonar Law. The latter divulged that not only had the individual himself been informed of his intended elevation, but that the Conservative Association in his constituency had been told that their Member was about to move to a higher place and that a by-election would be held immediately. "I cannot conceal from you", wrote Lord Stamfordham to Mr. Lloyd George, "that His Majesty was surprised and hurt that this honour should have been offered without first obtaining his consent. The King recognizes (in view of the promises made and information given) that it is impossible for him now to withhold his approval. But in thus signifying his acquiescence, His Majesty commands me to say he feels that the Sovereign's prerogative should not be disregarded; and he trusts that in future no honours whatever will be offered by any Minister until his approval has been informally obtained." '

The name of the 'Conservative Member representing a safe constituency' was, of course, Max Aitken, though Sir Harold Nicolson does not disclose this name.

Later the King objected to Lloyd George's appointment of Beaverbrook as Chancellor of the Duchy of Lancaster and Minister of Information. On 8 February 1918, Lord Stamfordham, the King's Secretary, wrote to the Chief Whip that His Majesty 'expressed much surprise that, considering past circumstances, he should now be asked to agree to Lord Beaverbrook's presiding over the Duchy which, as it were, is the personal property of the Sovereign and entailing closer relations between the King and its Chancellor than with many of his Ministers.'

Lloyd George stood firm in this appointment. But he and Aitken were soon at odds. Aitken, in the course of his duties as Minister of Information, would invite editors from Canada and America to come to Britain. Lloyd George, as Prime Minister, would not see these editors if Aitken made the request, but agreed to have them come to him when Lord Northcliffe, the powerful newspaper owner, demanded it.

At the end of August 1918 the following words appeared in an editorial in the *Daily Express*: 'If the Prime Minister [Lloyd George] seeks re-election as head of a Coalition Government, he must satisfy those who are to vote for him that his views and theirs are the same. . . . What, for instance, is the Prime Minister's programme on Tariff Reform and Imperial Preference? . . . Is the Welsh Church to be sacrificed simply because the party of Spoilers just tottering to its fall over the Irish Crisis of 1914 was saved for a moment by the outbreak of the Great War?'

This editorial was an embarrassment to Lloyd George, the Prime Minister. It went to the heart of his dilemma. Lloyd George had to try and keep the support of the Free Trade Liberals and also the Tories who wanted Tariff Reform on the election programme. Although Ministers (like Lord Beaverbrook) were under an obligation not to 'traffic with the Press' while they were in the Government, the editorial had all the marks of a deliberate attempt by Max Beaverbrook to make mischief.

Lloyd George wrote angrily to Bonar Law, 'Have you seen the leader in today's *Daily Express*? That is Max. Having regard to the risks I ran for him and the way I stood up for him when he was attacked by his own party, I regard this as a mean piece of treachery. It explains why no man in any party trusts Max. The reference to the Welsh Church is deliberately introduced to make it impossible for me to arrange matters with the Unionist [Tory] leaders. I am sorry, for I have sincerely tried to work with him.'

Churchill was sent by Lloyd George to see Beaverbrook. (Churchill was now back in the Government as Minister of Munitions.) Churchill said, 'The Prime Minister wants to know if you inspired that editorial in the *Daily Express*'. Beaverbrook replied, 'I did'.

Churchill said he would be sorry to have to take such an answer back to the Prime Minister, who would certainly ask for Beaverbrook's resignation. Beaverbrook said, 'Take it'.

Churchill repeated this conversation to Lloyd George who said, 'Oh well, we'll have to think about it'. And he did no more about it, except to tell others, 'It was all Freddie Guest's fault'. (Freddie Guest, a cousin of Winston Churchill, was Chief Whip for the Government at that time.)

At the end of October 1918 Beaverbrook had actinomycosis. He resigned from office. He said then, and until he died, that he felt like a prisoner freed from ball and chain.

He used his freedom in the next four years to help break Lloyd George's Coalition, bring Bonar Law out of retirement and make him Prime Minister of Britain before his death. It happened this way.

In March 1921, with Lloyd George still Prime Minister of the Coalition Government that had won the post-war election, Bonar Law resigned as Lord Privy Seal, Leader of the House of Commons, and Leader of the Tory Party on the grounds of ill-health.

Austen Chamberlain replaced him as Party Leader in the House of Commons.

By the middle of next year, 1922, there was rising dissatisfaction with Lloyd George's policies and leadership in the ranks of the Conservatives. Some wanted to pull out of the

Coalition and pull it down. Others, like Austen Chamberlain, wanted to stay with Lloyd George and uphold him.

A Carlton Club meeting of the Tory M.P.s to decide these vital matters was called for 19 October.

The 18th of October was a fateful day. Sir Archibald Salvidge, the powerful political Tory boss of Liverpool and confidant of Lord Derby, who wished the Coalition to continue, told Bonar Law and Birkenhead (according to Randolph Churchill in his official biography of the late Lord Derby called *Lord Derby, 'King of Lancashire'*, p. 464), 'Much of the demand for a change of Government had been engineered by Lord Beaverbrook because, though until recently a Coalition supporter, he had failed to exercise over the present Cabinet the influence he desired on behalf of certain oil interests in the East'.

Birkenhead repeated this to Beaverbrook. Beaverbrook had no oil interests in the East and was angry. That evening Salvidge went to see Bonar Law at his home in Onslow Gardens. Salvidge records, 'He spoke in the saddest and most gentle way. He had finally and definitely made up his mind to go to the Carlton Club meeting the next day, speak in favour of ending the Coalition and indicate his willingness to resume the leadership and form an independent Conservative Government.'

Salvidge reminded him of a day in Downing Street, soon after the First World War ended, when Bonar Law had said of Lloyd George, 'We must never let the little man go. His ways and ours lie side by side in the future.'

Bonar Law flushed deeply. Salvidge then said that Lloyd George had the 'unswerving support of every one of his Conservative colleagues in the Cabinet'.

A servant had come in during this interview and given a message to Bonar Law. Bonar Law puffed at his pipe for a few moments. At last he said, almost regretfully, without the slightest note of triumph in his voice, 'I may as well tell you that Lord Curzon is here. He is waiting in another room.'

Curzon was Lloyd George's Tory Foreign Minister. He was a notorious political trimmer. He had solemnly promised Asquith to sustain him in 1916, and then left him for Lloyd George. Now he was about to do the same to Lloyd George.

When Salvidge carried these dark tidings to Downing Street where Lloyd George awaited news, somebody remarked, 'So our punctilious pro-consul has ratted, has he?' The 'pro-consul' was a reference to the fact that Curzon had been made Viceroy of India at the early age of thirty-nine, and had been unable to recover on this earth from such a foretaste of celestial happiness. His crest has been described as a 'popinjay rising with wings extended'. Underneath his coronet lived a political chameleon. Under his peacock's feathers fluttered the mythical bulbul bird which flies backwards in stormy weather to keep its seat cool. Except that Lord Curzon's object was always to keep a seat in the Cabinet warm.

Late that night, 18 October, Bonar Law authorized Beaverbrook to tell the Press Association he was going to the Carlton Club meeting next day. He went, took a strong line, and Chamberlain was defeated by an overwhelming majority. Lloyd George and his Coalition fell.

Bonar Law led the Conservatives to victory at a General Election. And he was Prime Minister until his sudden illness a few months later and his death in 1923 from cancer of the throat.

Of Beaverbrook's part in all these events, Randolph Churchill gives this assessment in his book on Lord Derby (pp. 452, 453):

'The prime mover and principal agent in the plan to bring down the Coalition Government was Beaverbrook. . . . He had played a leading part behind the scenes in the election of Bonar Law in 1911 as Leader of the Conservative Party upon the resignation of Arthur Balfour. He had been active in the formation of the first Coalition Government under Asquith and he had probably done more than anyone else except Lloyd

George to pull Asquith down and to set up Lloyd George in his place. Anyone who has read the chronicles of these times and has had the opportunity to discuss them with the leading figures, cannot doubt that the decisive responsibility in persuading Bonar Law to come to the Carlton Club and announce his return to public life, was Beaverbrook.'

5

PEERAGE AND PRESS

Beaverbrook the Newspaperman

AITKEN'S journey to Paradise, his uplifting to the panoplied purple of the House of Lords, was always resented by a man who had both feet so firmly on the ground. He once said, 'No sooner had I fallen into a place in the hereditary system than the absurdity and futility of the political structure of the House of Lords became clear to me. Certainly I had no respect for the aristocracy as such, and no lingering admiration for the doings of the Squire and his family.'

My own belief is that the House of Lords is an invaluable political asset to this country. I do not speak of the hereditary system. I speak of men (nowadays, I suppose, of women too), many of whom have spent a lifetime in public service, who have grown wise in the ways of humanity and in the use or misuse of power, who are able to speak in honesty in the House of Lords without looking constantly over their shoulders to see how voters are receiving their views.

The standard of speaking in the House of Lords is far higher than in the House of Commons. Often, you hear more common sense there. And much legislation, hurried or thrust through the Commons, is polished and pruned in the Lords. It becomes better legislation.

There seems to me nothing but value in having a House of Lords with power to introduce new laws to the land, but without any power whatever to prevent for any length of time the Commons from doing what the people will in the life of the nation.

One thing more. Laws have been passed allowing a man to disempeer himself. For it is said that a Peer would no longer be acceptable as Prime Minister of Britain. If true, this seems foolish. Most Cabinet men nowadays give the appearance of lacking time to think. There is too much exercise of the tongue and too little of the brain. They are overborne with a mass of detail. It would be a first-rate experiment to have a Peer as Prime Minister, a man not forced each day to the tiring and sometimes petty questionings and oratory of the Commons, but with time to think out and give Britain the theme and goal of nationhood the country lacks and needs. What is wrong is the snobbery in human hearts which makes men treat a Peer as if he were by divine right more important than a postman or a publican. But the Peers cannot be blamed for the false values of snobbery in those who wear no coronet. Even though many of them enjoy the ration of lard and soap that some serve them.

Beaverbrook in later years did not play too active a part in the House of Lords. This was the country's loss. Nevertheless, I am glad he was ennobled. Not because it prevented him from going to the pinnacle of politics, but because it freed more of his energies for the Press. He once declared, 'Journalism is the most fascinating of all professions'.

It is fashionable in some quarters to sneer at the *Express*. The Duke of Edinburgh put it in his own striking style when he told a group in Latin America, 'The *Daily Express* is a bloody awful newspaper'.

Of course, the Duke would not have felt able to give so robust and profound a verdict unless he read the paper with care. This is more honest than Baldwin. Baldwin boasted he never read the *Express*. In truth it was almost always the first paper he picked up in the smoke-room of the House of Commons.

For my part, I am one of more than ten million who read it every day. It has done more for this country than many of those who criticize it. At times when the country risks losing faith in herself, the *Express* carries a candle of hope amid the gloom.

Hope, like the gleaming taper's light,
Adorns and cheers our way,
And still, as darker grows the night,
Emits a brighter ray.

And, in its practice and preachment of high wages, it has benefited and affected the economic and social condition of millions of people in this land more closely than they yet know. And in the last forty years the *Express* has done more to increase wages, improve working conditions, and alter the attitudes of privilege and power than most of its Left-Wing assailants.

One column in the *Express* is called 'Opinion'. So I can give mine. The *Express* was Beaverbrook. Beaverbrook was the *Express*. Do not misunderstand me. The *Express* is bigger than any man who works for it, including its proprietor. That is true of most successful organizations. It will continue to march ahead long after those who now produce it have met their last deadlines and come to an eternal halt. Beaverbrook seems to have passed on to his son Max and other *Express* executives the secret of surprise that is the genius of a popular newspaper. But I did not believe Lord Beaverbrook's statements, repeated time and again for thirty years, that he had nothing to do with the control of his newspapers. The truth is that he played a ceaseless part in their control. If he had not done so, the *Express* newspapers would never have possessed the crackle, bite, and spark that set them in the forefront.

In November 1928 Beaverbrook wrote:

'I have put eight years of my life into making the *Daily Express* whatever it is. I am the creator of the structure. . . . But my share in the work is now done. I am like a ship-builder who built a ship but will not be her captain. As the ship glides down the slipway, he says, "Farewell". I planned the *Daily Express*, but the staff are more competent than I am to manage it. . . . I can conceive and create, but I cannot conduct. . . . So on the very last day of the month of November 1927, I said good-bye to the *Daily Express* office for ever.'

It may have been sincere. But it was a lie notwithstanding. Beaverbrook remained skipper of the ship, boss of the boat, Viking of the vessel. Nor were his staff more competent than he. Nor was it true that he could not conduct. He was conductor, fiddler, trombonist, piccolo player, and double-bass all in one. He also sat with his feet cocked up in the gallery hooting or cheering his own performers as the mood struck him.

Carlyle said that genius is the transcendent capacity of taking trouble. If so, Beaverbrook was a genius of the Press. He worked. He worked harder than any man employed by him. He did so for years, and to the last. Do not believe pictures of him basking in the sunshine, taking his ease, a lolling Lordling of other men's labours, reaping their gain.

He worked in the morning.

He worked at night.

He worked when the moon shone down at midnight on his more personal life and when he strode breastforward with the multitude in the noonday sun.

He worked. Everything he said, heard, did was measured against its use for his Press.

The following is an account of a day in the life of Lord Beaverbrook from the book *The Londoner*, by Tudor Jenkins, who for more than twenty years edited the *Londoner's Diary* in Beaverbrook's *Evening Standard:*

'Lord Beaverbrook is a tremendous worker. His day begins early. By nine o'clock, when in London, he is on the telephone to the *Evening Standard* with his news and views after reading the morning papers.

'Always he is available for consultation. When he is given a piece of important information, his brain reacts like lightning. Immediately he will dictate back a paragraph of comment for the *Londoner's Diary* that is cinematic in its vividness—so good that it can go into the paper without alteration.

'In fact, he does not like his phraseology to be altered. That is why his editors always switch on a tape-recorder when they speak to Beaverbrook on the telephone. I have known days when the whole of the *Diary* has come from him. On those occasions his comment would be: "You have a fine *Diary* tonight."

'In the afternoons and evenings he is concerned with his other papers, the *Daily Express* and the *Sunday Express*. He keeps so close to the heart of things that it is a very rare thing for him to lunch or dine out. He prefers to have his friends at his own home, so that he does not lose touch at all with his papers.

'Beaverbrook is a stickler for style and accuracy. He abominates clichés.

'Picture the scene in the study of his penthouse flat in Arlington House, St. James's. Here he stands before a lectern reading articles and memoranda submitted by his editors. Beside him is a tape-recorder into which he speaks his verdicts and comments.

'When he has finished with them, Beaverbrook screws the articles into balls. They have to be cleared several times a day.

'It is while standing at his lectern that Beaverbrook goes through his newspapers as they reach him from Fleet Street. Features in which he has particular interest he reads line by line, sliding a sheet of foolscap down the printed page to guide his eye.

'Should he find an inaccuracy or a cliché, he barks a reprimand into the microphone of his voice-recorder. If he finds a story particularly well done, he sends a message congratulating the writer. Sometimes he finds that the writer is a young journalist of whom he has never heard before. Beaverbrook will send for him and speak words of encouragement and advice to the beginner.'

Beaverbrook breakfasted at seven. He kept a pad beside him at every meal, and took notes all through the day. The Psalmist says, 'If riches increase, set not your heart upon them.

. . . Thou Lord art merciful, for Thou rewardest every man according to his work'. If it is possible for any man to be said to have earned wealth of the kind Beaverbrook possessed, then it is true to say he earned every penny of it.

And he built the most lively newspaper in Britain.

Divisive—often. Damnable—frequently. Dynamite—always. Dull—never.

Beaverbrook bought a controlling interest in the *Daily Express* on 2 December 1916. It was the Saturday before Asquith's resignation from the Premiership. Beaverbrook bought the paper as a weapon to sustain Bonar Law and his own Imperial viewpoint. He made no secret of it. More than thirty years later he told the Royal Commission on the Press, 'I run the paper purely for the purpose of making propaganda, and for no other motive'.

In *Politicians and the Press*, published in 1925, he tells how he bought it.

'I had for a number of years a considerable connection with the *Daily Express* of an indefinite character, but it never interested me much. Towards the end of the war that newspaper wanted money very urgently to keep up its supply of newsprint. None of its shareholders would put up any money. Finally the Editor came to me and suggested that I could purchase the controlling shares in the newspaper for £17,500. Of course, such a purchase implied not merely finding the necessary sum for the purchase of newsprint, but the financial responsibility for the newspaper as a whole.

'I hesitated. But a merciful delay was given me by the fact that I was placed in quarantine as a "carrier" of spino-meningitis germs. When I was released, I went on a black Saturday winter's evening to consult Lord Rothermere on the venture. His summing up amounted to this: To buy the shares of this concern at the price offered implied a good deal of courage. To do so meant the supply not only of a considerable amount of money in addition to the price of purchase, but also in the long run the expenditure of a good deal of time and energy in looking after the business. I asked him whether he would take a share in the enterprise, but he explained that he could not do this, as it would involve competing with his brother, Lord Northcliffe, as owner of the *Daily Mail*. Nonetheless he advised me to accept the offer—and I did.'

The net circulation of the *Daily Express* was at that time 229,344. Today it is around 4,400,000. The property, bought for £17,500, has a market value now of many millions. Northcliffe, Rothermere's brother, was also consulted by Beaverbrook before he bought the *Express*. Northcliffe was said to know everything about newspapers. He asked Beaverbrook, 'How much are you worth?' Beaverbrook said, 'Over five million dollars'. Northcliffe said, 'You will lose it all in Fleet Street'.

Northcliffe was wrong.

Beaverbrook founded the *Sunday Express* on 29 December 1918. It lost £150,000 the first year, £300,000 the second year. Its circulation fell from its starting point of 300,000 to 155,000. But today its circulation is over 4,400,000.

Many men have played a part in this success. Many have tipped their talents into the common pot and from it drawn in their time a pot of gold. But while other men have been allowed to get in the driving seat, Beaverbrook supplied the fuel and the map. He was the speed-cop and always encouraged the driver to go faster.

Reasons for the success of the Beaverbrook newspapers seem clear.

1. The *Express* is a paper with a theme and a goal. It is a fighting paper. It is a paper which knows what it stands for and loves what it knows. And whether or not others love its aims, at least they know them. Every young man likes a fight. The *Express* goes not cap but sword in hand, knocking at the gateways of the great. It may not win every campaign. But it wins many. And in that struggle its own position has been established.

2. Its owner could not draw cartoons. But he could do every editorial job, except cartooning, in his papers as well as the man doing it at the desk. That is not so of other newspaper owners. But Beaverbrook, with his muscle of mind and pen, could write, edit, get news, sell advertising, hire and fire as well as the rest of them rolled into one. In the space of two hours, when he was eighty-three, I heard him dictate two editorials, question the size of the Scottish edition of his newspaper, dictate three important letters, speak to the editors of two of his newspapers, discuss business details, involving many complicated figures, with the General Manager of the *Express* group, and give orders for meals and the entertainment of guests in his home.

He took care in all the details of his life at the office and in his home. He would send a memo to the chef, 'The beef was tough. Tell me why.' And to the leader writer, 'Too many adjectives in that column today. Don't waste words.'

His prose style was his own. It could not be mistaken. The sections of the editorial columns which he wrote himself could be recognized.

He asked his friend Rudyard Kipling to teach him to write. Kipling did so. Kipling's own method was to write what he had in mind, put it away for several weeks, then go over it with a paint-brush and Indian ink, painting out every unnecessary word. He would then put it away again and, after another interval, take the paint-brush over it a second time. By then it was pruned for print.

Beaverbrook could not, from the nature of the daily Press, wait weeks to polish his prose. But he kept the short sentences and the frugality of words that he learned at Kipling's feet. He wrote books as well as articles in later years. They are books of high literary as well as historical merit.

His sense of fun was swift and sparkles through his Press. Two stories show something of his power of retort. He was speaking in Glasgow where the new prison is called Barlinnie.

There was much heckling at this meeting. One heckler kept

on shouting, 'There is no unemployment in Russia'. Beaverbrook had just been in Russia. The audience therefore insisted on him giving his views on unemployment in that land. Beaverbrook said, 'No. There is no unemployment in Russia.' His opponents in the audience cheered long and loud. Beaverbrook asked to say something else. When silence fell, he remarked, 'There is no unemployment in Russia. There is no unemployment in Barlinnie Prison. But I would not like to be there.'

On another occasion Lady Cunard came to see Beaverbrook. She was a close friend of Sir Thomas Beecham. Indeed, she desired to marry him. 'It takes two to make a marriage,' Beaverbrook said, 'and I don't think Tom would have been a willing bridegroom.' Lady Cunard asked Beaverbrook's help in seeing that the Buckmaster Bill, relating to divorce, became the law of the land. She believed the Bill would ease her road to wedding Sir Thomas. She said, 'If that Bill doesn't pass, I'll commit suicide'. An obstacle to her marriage plans was her husband, Sir Bache Cunard. Beaverbrook replied, 'Why not try murder first?' Lady Cunard did not find the joke at all funny.

3. Beaverbrook had the power to help men grow and give their best at their labours. The story that it was a frail and hazardous life in the *Express* was only true if you suffered from the modern malady of wanting more and more in return for less and less. You would get more and more all right. In the seven years I worked for Beaverbrook my salary multiplied by five. I did not once ask for a rise in pay. When I started work with him, I was certainly worth far less than he paid me. The same is probably true when I left him.

Beaverbrook paid hard cash, but expected hard work. In the last year of my time on the *Express* newspapers I was doing leaders for the *Daily Express* and the *Evening Standard* each day —and for the *Sunday Express* on Sunday. I was writing a signed political column each week. I was writing articles on Society under the name of Captain Barnabe Rich. (He was a cad. He discussed men's wages, women's ages, the hidden habits of the Establishment with candour and delight. Many false rumours about his identity were circulated around London clubs by Beaverbrook and others like myself. When the demand for truth became too strong we published a photograph of a Moss Bros. advertisement in the middle of Captain Rich's column, a distinguished man in a grey top hat and morning coat, and under it was the caption, 'Captain Barnabe Rich goes to the races'.) I wrote serious articles under the name Adan Bothwell, contributed a children's daily feature called *Pindar the Panda*, illustrated by Low, to the *Evening Standard*, discussed farming under the pen-name of Brent Ely.

When I left the *Express* building for the last time, about ten men clattered downstairs and out into the Fleet Street traffic with me. I lived, slept, breathed, snored, and dreamed for my work.

But once when I was pushed by a multitude of duties, Beaverbrook sent for me. It was three o'clock in the afternoon. He said, 'Now I've had an idea for an article. And here it is.' I was tired. I was overloaded. One more article was more than I could bear. My bitterness must have showed in my face. I pulled what my loved nurse in my childhood used to call a 'bunny-nose'. It means folding your lips with sullenness and lengthening your nostrils with disdain.

Beaverbrook at once set aside his papers and took off his spectacles. He said, quietly but passionately, 'Now, look here, Peter. I don't pay you your money to sulk. If you want to sulk, go somewhere else to do it. If you want to work, stick with me. Otherwise get out.'

I stuck. I learned the lesson of giving your best no matter how you feel. It is a lesson beyond price in life. Much smithying makes a man a smith. And Beaverbrook gave everybody a good chance to become a master of the craft. At the same time, he was prone to treat those who worked closely with him as sons, not as hired servants. He was a goad and gold man. He put a goad in men's pants and gold in their pockets.

The best proof of him as a boss is the men who stayed with him rather than those who left. Many have spent their working lives in his service and in it have found fulfilment.

The old sage urged man, 'Know thyself'. It's a hard thing to do. Beaverbrook helped many men to know what they can work at—and to work at it. Sir Frederick Doidge, later Foreign Minister of New Zealand and High Commissioner for his country in London, was trained by Beaverbrook in Fleet Street. He said to me one day, 'Stick with Max. He'll make you a great man.' I did not. And he could not. But it is true that those who stuck with Max are greater than most of those who left him.

4. The *Express* newspapers sell on news. Stories like the flight of Burgess and Maclean might never have come to the daylight without Beaverbrook's men. Story after story of modern man is first told in its pages. News sells newspapers—and the *Express* seeks it and gives it.

5. The *Express* is a paper of youth. Beaverbrook, in his old age, still had the gift of being gentle with the weak and tough with the strong. It is a rare combination. Young men were constantly being pushed to the front in the *Express* newspapers. You could hear Beaverbrook saying to his latest 'find', 'Yes. Yes. You did that very well indeed. But let me make this suggestion to you . . .' These suggestions were a lifetime of experience in the Craft of Ink if the young man had the grace and sense to see it.

Beaverbrook did not make the mistake so many other newspapermen have made. He did not do it all himself. He spent much of his lifetime training others.

Whatever the future holds, some stamp of character was made by Beaverbrook on the papers he controlled that will prove permanent.

Mr. John Beavan, former Editor of the *Daily Herald* and at

present political adviser to the *Mirror* group, says, 'Sociologically, the *Express* is the most interesting paper of all. . . . It is the closest thing to the classless or all-class paper that we have in the daily field.'

Francis Williams wrote recently in the *New Statesman* (7 February 1964): 'The *Express* owes its astonishing success over the years to a formula which, however much one may regret it, has appealed to a wider cross-section of national society than any other newspaper in history. As a newspaper proprietor Lord Beaverbrook has bridged all class distinctions to a degree no one has ever succeeded in doing before.'

And one other feature of the *Express* is likely to endure. Beaverbrook was a son of the manse. In all the mud and slime, the skulduggery and jiggerypokery of modern life, he never forgot it. Sex, crime, violence, all play their part in the news of the day. The *Express*, with its massive circulation and mighty success, has not used a muck-heap to climb upon. It is a family paper still.

Yet this hatred of pornography sometimes seems a pose. The cry against it is so shrill, the abuse of it so vehement that it becomes an affectation. The notes of this bell, which rings so loud and long across the nation from the roof of the Black Glass Building in Fleet Street, have from time to time an over-strident, artificial, forced clang. There is a crack in the bell somewhere.

Nevertheless, you will not find pornography in the Beaverbrook Press.

Prejudice, yes, but not pornography. Viewpoints, yes, but not vice.

In Britain today four-letter words have become the fashion. God, a three-letter word, is out of style.

But in the columns of the *Express*, four-letter words are still out, and God still finds His way in.

6

MAX B., STANLEY B.

Beaverbrook the Enemy

LORD BEAVERBROOK had two dogs. They were chows with black tongues, black hearts, and ginger hair and hide. Their names were Brendan and Brunswick. They were square-heads, but not squares. They were mutinous and gay.

Beaverbrook took pains to train these animals. As he rode with a friend through the yew forest that girdled his Surrey home, the dogs would be led by long leads between the horses. Often they sat on their rumps and were dragged, sled-like and yowling over the earth. They were fed by Beaverbrook himself. Beaverbrook would say with awe as the dogs gobbled from the dish he placed before them, 'Look at them, Just look at them. I'm their god.'

One day a friend of mine, a man with a pen of power, was laughing so heartily in a Fleet Street pub that he spilt the drink he was holding. This stopped his laughter. Then he told me, 'Do you know, one of those damned dogs has bitten Max!'

That evening he and I were asked to dine with Beaverbrook. The bite of the dog, when Beaverbrook showed it to us, was not severe. It was a thin fillet of flesh torn from his wrist. But as Beaverbrook told the story, I began to laugh myself. Beaverbrook thought I was laughing at him. In truth I was laughing at the looks of grief and exclamations of concern which came from my friend in Lord Beaverbrook's presence and which were so different from his delight and glee in the pub in Fleet Street.

Beaverbrook was more hurt by the dog's ingratitude than by its teeth. He had an instinctive desire to control. He had the capacity to handle great affairs. He had a lifelong conviction about where this nation should go. It was natural for a man with the impulsion of the gift of strong leadership within him to want to use it to the full. He would have liked to control and lead Britain as he led his dogs on horseback through the Cherkley yew forest. He controlled some men by money, others by flattery, others by force of personality. But Baldwin was the dog who bit him.

Baldwin was the most powerful political figure in Britain from 1923 until 1937. Throughout that time, he led the Conservative Party. For most of the time, he was Prime Minister. They were years when Britain passed from a pinnacle of strength to a pit of danger.

Beaverbrook, for much of that time, did his best to control Baldwin or to destroy him. In both aims he failed.

If all the good people were clever,
  And all clever people were good,
The world would be nicer than ever
  We thought that it possibly could.

But somehow, 'tis seldom or never
  The two hit it off as they should;
The good are so harsh to the clever,
  The clever so rude to the good!

Baldwin and Beaverbrook, Beaverbrook and Baldwin. Which was clever? Which was good? It is certainly true that Beaverbrook was often rude to Baldwin. And Baldwin was sometimes harsh to Beaverbrook. The truth is that both men were in different degrees clever.

Nowadays, the story is told that Beaverbrook held a vendetta against Baldwin which he followed with mischief, rancour,

Notwithstanding, Beaverbrook sincerely shared the attitude of those Presbyterians who say marriage is nothing but a contract.

It was this view of the marriage-vows, differing from that held by Catholics and many Episcopalians, that, as much as any other reason, added acid to the struggle between Beaverbrook and Baldwin's men which ended in the abdication of the Duke of Windsor.

Baldwin asked me to go and see him in his Worcestershire home after he had left Downing Street and I had left Fleet Street. I often had stabbed him with my pen. Also, he knew I had played a part in writing *Guilty Men*, a book which denounced him.

He was polite to me. He told me that he held Beaverbrook responsible for all my shortcomings of the past. When I told him that I owed a debt to Beaverbrook, for personal kindness that went far beyond what was needed in training me to handle pen and men, Lord Baldwin said, fiercely snapping his fingers in the air, 'Preparing the tool. Preparing the tool.' Though hardly flattering to my self-esteem, I realized my host believed that Beaverbrook's only use for a man like myself had been as a sharpened stooge to poke the flanks of a man like himself. It became clear that Lord Baldwin hoped I would indulge in a denunciation of Lord Beaverbrook, which would satisfy some longing to stab the Baron of the Press.

Baldwin told me that Churchill wanted him to broadcast to the people. Churchill felt that the man whose motto had been 'Safety First' in peace could become 'Safety Last' in war. 'But I shall not do it', he said. 'It will do nothing but harm for me to open my mouth now. In the future people will see I was right. But now I must stay silent.'

He again spoke of Beaverbrook and appeared in some measure to blame him for the disfavour into which he had fallen. He said, 'I disliked him from the first moment I saw him. Years ago I told some people that I would not put my feet under the same table with Beaverbrook. One of them went off and repeated it to him. He has never forgiven me—and I still wouldn't put my feet under the table with him.' Beaverbrook's attacks on Baldwin were mostly public. Baldwin's attacks on Beaverbrook were mostly private. But Baldwin pursued Beaverbrook with skill, hostility, and subtlety year in and year out, and damaged his image within the Establishment far more effectively than Beaverbrook succeeded in damaging Baldwin before the people of the land.

Baldwin told me that Beaverbrook had been an evil influence with Bonar Law. 'And I'm afraid he is the same with Winston Churchill', he added. He said that whenever Beaverbrook fell ill, he heard the flames of hell roaring for him and thought of the harm he had done to Baldwin. 'When he is dying, he will send for me and try to put things right', he told me. I asked if he would go. He shrugged and grunted, but made no answer.

My last memory of him is a sad one. I see him standing in the doorway of his Worcestershire home bidding me farewell and saying twice, more, as it seemed, to reassure himself than to give me information, 'I still have friends, you know. I still have friends at Westminster.'

It is an irony of life that Baldwin owed his first step upwards in politics to Beaverbrook. Bonar Law wanted a Secretary. Beaverbrook recommended Baldwin and Bonar Law took him on. The reason for the choice was not on account of any personal achievement, but because Baldwin was rich, could entertain and make friends for his master, and was, they thought, easy to control.

Bechover Roberts records in his *Stanley Baldwin, Man or Miracle?*, that Baldwin was chosen because he was 'discreet enough to be "safe" and "stupid" enough not to intrigue'. Beaverbrook believed things changed after Baldwin got his first job. He recorded his view: 'Up to the outbreak of war [1914] he showed not the slightest trace of political push or ambition. . . . On attaining to junior office, his character changed. Ambition marked him. Thereafter came a steady development of growing powers.'

The first big Front Bench speech Baldwin made as Government spokesman was as Financial Secretary to the Treasury in 1918. He strongly defended the Minister of Information, Lord Beaverbrook, then under attack. In the course of his remarks, Baldwin said, 'He is a man of strong personality. Men with strong personalities have this in common—that the magnetism which comes with that personality either attracts or repels.' And shortly before the Armistice in 1918, when Beaverbrook, because of a temporary failure in health, resigned his Government post, Baldwin spoke in Parliament of his 'rare vision'.

When Bonar Law got cancer of the throat and resigned the Premiership in 1923, after winning a majority of seventy-one seats for the Conservatives at the 1922 General Election, in Beaverbrook's own words, 'Something was severed for ever in my political associations. I had never cared much for the purely political life, but Bonar Law's charm, his urbanity, his wisdom, his firm and reasonable attitude towards all problems, held me like a silken chain.'

There was a struggle for power. Lord Curzon of Kedleston, former Viceroy of India, a man who would scorn to be called a bird of paradise because he felt equipped to govern all the earth and possibly Paradise as well, against Stanley Baldwin, the wealthy country Squire.

Bonar Law was not asked to make any recommendation and indeed did not make any recommendation as to his successor. Curzon was so sure of his triumph that when he heard King George V had sent for Baldwin, he wept and declared again and again, 'Baldwin? Baldwin? A man of the utmost insignificance.'

But it is worth remembering that at that supreme moment in the life of Baldwin, Beaverbrook and his Press gave him their support. He won. The man came to power whose political battles with Beaverbrook, the bloodshed, the blows above and below the belt, the fouls and the clinches when the two combatants hugged and panted and glared at each other for a while before falling to it again, enlivened the political arena for a generation.

They tell a tale of smugglers.

A lady entering the country from abroad informed the Customs Officer she had nothing to declare.

A respectable-looking gentleman standing near by at once said, 'That's a lie. I feel it my duty to let you know that I overheard this lady on board our ship boasting that she was going to smuggle a watch into the country.'

The lady was searched. The watch was found. Police were called. The watch was confiscated. The gentleman was praised for his sense of public duty. And a summons was issued against the lady.

On the train to London she came face to face with the man who had informed against her. She spat with rage. She said it was no business of his. But what saddened her most was the loss of her watch.

The man politely rolled up his sleeve and, showing her twenty smuggled watches strapped around his arm, said, 'Madam, take your pick'.

Beaverbrook was the lady who got found out—Baldwin the respectable gentleman who gave such accurate information against her. Baldwin used to say Beaverbrook had dirty hands. Beaverbrook would hold up his hands at public meetings and cry, 'Look. They are clean.'

One of the charges which Baldwin laid at Beaverbrook's door was that the Press Lord had tried to meddle with the Premier's prerogative of Cabinet making. It arose when a gentleman called Lord Murray of Elibank gave his views to Baldwin that Beaverbrook would make peace if he could have two of his men in the Cabinet.

Beaverbrook knew nothing of this approach. Nothing at all. But Baldwin chose to believe that Elibank was Beaverbrook's emissary. He described the approach as a demand from Fleet Street to pick members of the Cabinet. Misunderstandings multiplied.

The truth is that Beaverbrook was always a 'doer'. He wanted things done. He wanted them done in a hurry. He was against those who wanted things left much as they were and, if they had to be altered, then altered slowly.

Baldwin was by nature indolent and optimistic. 'The sooner it's over, the sooner to sleep' was his way of life.

Long before Baldwin came to power and prominence, the hard-core hierarchy of the Tory Party distrusted the drive of Beaverbrook—and where he was driving.

As early as 1921 Beaverbrook was fighting the hierarchy over an embargo on Canadian cattle. He supported a candidate at a by-election at Dudley who beat the Minister of Agriculture, Sir A. G. Boscawen. Boscawen supported the embargo. Beaverbrook was a friend of Boscawen. He gave him the chance to let in the cattle, but when he refused, helped to throw him out of Parliament.

Beaverbrook, who in later years heard his own newspapers denounced in strong terms for bad taste by the Tory hierarchy, had to submit to this from the *Morning Post:*

Benefits Forgot

Lord Beaverbrook, your accents rude
Reveal a gross ingratitude.
'Tis true that hither none may bring
Canadian beasts for fattening.
Whoever may that rule arraign,
The last should you be to complain.
'Tis our affair, not yours to rue
That, spite of law, they let you through.

The Times refused to print Beaverbrook's name, referring to him as a 'gentleman from Canada'.

The Committee of the Carlton Club tried to expel Beaverbrook. They said he had broken a by-law which declared that members of the club should not oppose each other at by-elections. Both Boscawen and Beaverbrook were members. Of the club committee of fifteen, fourteen voted against Beaverbrook, one in his favour. Beaverbrook's sin was not that he had opposed Boscawen, but that he had beaten him.

Beaverbrook refused to be expelled. The committee said, 'You must'.

It was like the conflict in the heart of Gobbo. 'Budge', says the Fiend. 'Budge not', says my conscience.

In the end, Beaverbrook told the committee that he would fight them in the courts of law. The committee retreated and refused the challenge of the courts. 'So they won in the end', says Beaverbrook. 'I stayed on twenty years, paying my fees all the time—and scarcely went near the place.'

In fact, later the Carlton Club gave Beaverbrook a complimentary dinner. They presented him with a piece of plate. 'I left my car outside the club at that dinner', says Beaverbrook. 'A lorry crashed into it. Luckily the car was empty, but it was destroyed.'

It can be seen from this sort of row with the Carlton Club that the elements in the nation who later were known as 'Baldwin's men' were against the dynamo quality of Beaverbrook long before he attacked the dinosaur quality of Baldwin.

7

BELOW THE BELT

Beaverbrook the Boxer

THE ring was now built for the Empire heavyweight title between the two B.s. The first round was over the American Debt Settlement.

This arose from the money Britain owed America at the end of World War I. The European nations owed Britain more than Britain owed America. The British Prime Minister, Bonar Law, was clear that the wise and just course from the British, and from every viewpoint, was for a general, all-round, debt settlement. He inherited this policy from Lloyd George, his predecessor in the Premiership, and from Sir Robert Horne, Lloyd George's Chancellor of the Exchequer. Stanley Baldwin was sent by Bonar Law to America as the new Chancellor of the Exchequer with no authority to come to terms by himself, and with clear Cabinet instructions to discourage direct Anglo-American settlement unless the European debt to us was settled at the same time.

At the end of 1922, Bonar Law said in an interview, 'If I sign the terms suggested at Washington, I shall be the most cursed man in England'.

Suddenly the Cabinet heard that Baldwin was doing in Washington precisely what he had been told not to do. Cables were sent. Baldwin came home in a hurry. And stepping off the boat at Southampton, before seeing the Cabinet, he told the Press the terms of the suggested American settlement and said that in his view they should be accepted.

Bonar Law was so enraged by this disclosure, which to the mind of most people in this country and America meant that Britain had accepted America's terms, that he wished to resign from the Premiership. Only the pleas of his friends prevented it.

Baldwin later said he would sooner have bitten off his tongue than spoken as he did to the Press at Southampton. Whether his tongue was in his cheek when he said this, he alone knew. Certainly, though the Cabinet gnashed their teeth, Baldwin's tongue stayed whole, and active.

Beaverbrook vigorously and ceaselessly attacked the arrangement. It was his first full-scale onslaught on Baldwin. But the deal was done. Baldwin had in fact committed us in Washington to the settlement. The European nations defected in their payments to Britain while Britain staggered forward for years under the burden of the American debt.

The figures were as follows: At the end of World War I, Britain was owed by other countries £3,400,000,000. She owed America £850,000,000. Other countries were freed from, or defaulted in, payment of their debts to Britain.

Britain paid £326,000,000 to America. Her share of the total debt owing to America at the end of World War I was 40 per cent. Her share of the total repayment of the debt to America was 82 per cent.

Baldwin became Prime Minister for the first time after Bonar Law's retirement in May 1923.

Beaverbrook was asked to dinner with the Baldwins by J. C. C. Davidson, a crony of the Prime Minister. He found himself sitting next to Mrs. Baldwin, who said to him, 'You know, Stanley was betrayed by his friends who stuck knives in his back when he was in Washington settling the American debt'. The implication was that Beaverbrook had stabbed him. Beaverbrook made no reply.

Baldwin wanted to have an election. He invited Beaverbrook to Downing Street. At the door of Number 10, Beaverbrook met Mackenzie King of Canada. King had just seen Baldwin.

He told Beaverbrook that Baldwin was going to go to the country.

When Beaverbrook entered the room, he said to the Prime Minister, 'Is this going to be an Imperial Preference election?' Baldwin replied, 'No. I will only seek protection for certain industries in Britain—protection particularly against the Germans and their iron and steel output.'

Beaverbrook then told Baldwin plainly that he would not support him unless he incorporated Imperial Preference in his policies. He said that the Dominions must be brought into the sphere of Free Trade among themselves and protection against foreigners. The Prime Minister refused. He said, 'One day, perhaps. But not now. The country is not ready for any taxes on food. I will not impose duties on foreign foodstuffs with admission of Dominion foodstuffs duty-free.'

It was on that basis that Beaverbrook broke with Baldwin. At the 1923 election he helped finance twenty-five candidates who proclaimed Imperial Preference. Almost all of them were elected. Baldwin was defeated. The cry went up, 'Beaverbrook turned out the lights'.

Beaverbrook continued to agitate for Imperial Preference. When Winston Churchill fought the Abbey division of Westminster as an Independent candidate in 1924, Baldwin promised his support. But members of the local Tory party were against Churchill. They adopted the nephew of the late Member, an unknown and undistinguished man. So Baldwin withdrew his support of Churchill.

Beaverbrook, hearing Baldwin had withdrawn, supported Churchill with vigour. So did Balfour. So did Birkenhead. Beaverbrook says, 'Baldwin ran away. I stood to my guns for Winston.'

At that time Churchill was still a Free Trader. He was no more in favour of Imperial Preference than Baldwin. He had gone as far as Baldwin in accepting protection against imports of manufactured goods from the Continent. But he would go no further.

Nevertheless, with the support of Beaverbrook and his friends he came within forty-three votes of winning the Abbey division by-election against the official Conservative candidate, and the full force of the official Party machine.

Baldwin then attacked Beaverbrook and others.

On 18 May 1924 *The People* published an exclusive interview with Baldwin as leader of the Opposition. It was called 'the greatest political sensation in years'. Its headline was, 'Baldwin Turns and Rends his Critics'. Baldwin was reported as suggesting that it was he who risked everything in overthrowing Lloyd George's Coalition. Bonar Law, according to him, had told him only the day before the decisive Carlton Club meeting, where the Conservatives decided to quit the Lloyd George Coalition, that he was going to retire from politics. The implication was that when the Carlton Club meeting took place, Baldwin thought it was he himself, not Bonar Law, who would be in the lead.

Then, of Lord Birkenhead, Baldwin said, 'I am under no illusions as to Lord Birkenhead. If his health does not give way, he will be a liability to the Party. But can a leader in opposition shut the door to an ex-Minister?' (The reference to Lord Birkenhead's health was taken by everybody to mean that he was drinking too heavily. Beaverbrook used to declare that, contrary to popular legend and to the belief of many, Birkenhead was not addicted to the bottle. He drank—but Beaverbrook says he was not at the mercy of his habit.)

About Lord Beaverbrook (and Lord Rothermere), Baldwin said, 'For myself I do not mind these attacks. I care not what they say or think. They are both men that I would not have in my house. I do not respect them. Who are they? . . . The last time I spoke to Lord Beaverbrook was at Bonar Law's funeral. He had contracted a curious friendship with Bonar and had got his finger into the pie, where it had no business to be. He got hold of much information which he used in ways it was not intended. When I came in, that stopped. I know I could get support if I were to send for him and talk things over with him. But I prefer not. That sort of thing does not appeal to me. . . . What do these intriguers want? Simply to go back to the old dirty kind of politics. Not while I am leader of the Party.'

The Political Correspondent of *The People* ended his story with these words, 'And Mr. Baldwin yawned with disgust and weariness at discussing for so long so unpleasant a subject'.

No such attack had been made publicly before, nor has it been made since, by a political leader on colleagues inside his own party. There was an uproar. Baldwin took the simple course of denying that he had ever said any such things. He declared that the whole thing was a fabrication. He wrote a letter to each of the colleagues who felt they might have been libelled in the interview, in which he said, 'I hope you know me well enough to be certain that I never gave expression to the personal reflections on yourself which are there repeated. I am deeply distressed that I should have been so grossly misrepresented.' Beaverbrook made no reply. The others wrote accepting the disclaimer.

For a week every pressure of influence, coupled with threats of dismissal to journalists, was put upon the staff of *The People* to get them to withdraw the interview. The *Morning Post* added to the damage already done by printing in an editorial that there were 'some things which we should not wish unsaid, whether they were said by Mr. Baldwin or came from the fertile brain of the journalist'. The editorial added that there was 'so much truth in what he [Mr. Baldwin] is alleged to have said that it is almost as good as if he had said it'.

In spite of the pressures, *The People* stood firm. Next Sunday, 25 May 1924, it said that the interview had been arranged at the request of the Conservative Central Office so Baldwin could have a chance of replying to his critics. The paper added, 'The interview as printed is an adequate and accurate statement of the views and opinions expressed by Mr. Baldwin . . . the only exception is verbal changes which were made editorially as

The People could not take the responsibility for their publication'. The Political Correspondent declared that he had taken notes in full view of Baldwin. Behind the scenes, Beaverbrook, with his knowledge of the Press, and Birkenhead, with his sword-like lawyer's mind, were sure that the interview was genuine. So was Sir William Bull, at that time legal adviser to *The People*. A sentence like, 'He got hold of much information which he used in ways it was not intended' has the roughness of a man talking and thinking aloud rather than the polish of a skilled Fleet Street pen. From the objective viewpoint of forty years later, *The People*'s interview rings true.

Meanwhile, Baldwin worried because Beaverbrook alone refused to accept his claim that he had never said what *The People* reported. He learned of the possibility that Beaverbrook would issue a writ against him. He became alarmed. He got Sir Douglas Hogg to speak to Melville, who later became Solicitor-General. Melville asked Beaverbrook not to sue. Beaverbrook sent back word that he would have to do so. Baldwin thereupon sent Sam Hoare (later Lord Templewood) to see Beaverbrook. He begged Beaverbrook to come to Baldwin's home. Beaverbrook went.

There Baldwin made many apologies. He used all his charm—and he had charm. He went through the motions of good fellowship and asked Beaverbrook to treat the whole thing as a joke. He asked him not to issue the writ as such action would damage the Conservative Party greatly.

So Beaverbrook, who did not like lawsuits, agreed.

Before long, however, the attack in *The People* was repeated publicly by Ormsby-Gore (later Lord Harlech) who was a protégé of Baldwin and at that time a Junior Minister in Baldwin's Government. Ormsby-Gore declared he would stay in public life for the one aim of keeping Lloyd George, Churchill, and Beaverbrook out. He proposed himself as a bulwark against their influence in British affairs.

Lloyd George replied that Ormsby-Gore had not felt like

this when Lloyd George had been wartime Prime Minister. Ormsby-Gore at that time had sought office and held a job at 10 Downing Street. Lloyd George added that Ormsby-Gore was a great patriot who would follow the Flag anywhere—except into the front-line trenches.

Beaverbrook gave a softer answer. He wrote about this time in the *Sunday Express*, 'I never thought he [Baldwin] could be so good, or his Government so bad'.

Beaverbrook opposed Baldwin in the 1929 election because he proposed limited protection to protect British steel companies against German competition, but rejected Imperial Preference. After the 1929 Labour victory, support for Beaverbrook's campaign of Empire Free Trade grew in Britain. The allegation was made that Beaverbrook wished to supplant Baldwin as leader of the Tory Party. Beaverbrook replied, 'I will stand aside and obliterate myself from the movement, if the Conservative leader will announce . . . that he adopts our programme of Empire Free Trade'.

When rebuked for attacking Baldwin, Beaverbrook replied, 'This is not so. I have deliberately refrained from attacking him. . . . I have offered loyally to serve under him, subject, of course, to his adoption of the policies in which I so earnestly believe.' He added, however, 'We shall oppose every parliamentary candidate, no matter of which party, who does not adopt and further the policy of Empire Free Trade'.

This threat was carried out. In two days a fighting fund of £100,000 was raised for a new political party, the United Empire Party. Within a month, on 4 March 1930, Baldwin had made an Empire speech satisfactory to Beaverbrook, even if not going all the way. Thereupon the £100,000 was returned to those who had given it. A rally was organized at the Crystal Palace where Baldwin and Beaverbrook were to appear together. Baldwin had prepared a referendum to the nation on Imperial Preference.

On the day Beaverbrook agreed to the referendum, Baldwin

appeared at Stornoway House. It was in the afternoon. Baldwin said, 'You will be much criticized [for agreeing to Baldwin's referendum]. Many of your friends will say you have done wrong. But you have done right. We will be able to work together now.'

He left shaking hands. But within hours Beaverbrook felt he had been cheated. A Conservative Central Office leaflet appeared which retreated from the offer of a referendum.

The Crystal Palace rally was cancelled. It was announced that between sixty and a hundred Empire candidates would fight in constituencies in the south where either Labour or Conservative Members 'have not formally and expressly adhered to Lord Beaverbrook's leadership' on the matter of Imperial Preference.

Beaverbrook's candidate won a by-election at South Paddington. At East Islington, Beaverbrook's man nearly won again. Miss Thelma Cazalet (now Mrs. Cazalet-Keir) was Baldwin's candidate. Beaverbrook put up Brigadier Critchley, who destroyed Miss Cazalet and beat himself, too, splitting the Conservative vote and letting in the Socialists.

Now inside the Conservative Party a tide was running against Baldwin. Baldwin knew that a large section of his own party were moving in the direction of Beaverbrook's policies and away from his own tactics of delay. At that point, the first Lord Rothermere, who was supporting Beaverbrook in his bid for leadership, placed a deadly weapon in the hands of Baldwin.

At a Caxton Hall meeting on 24 June 1930 Baldwin adjusted his spectacles and read to a concourse of M.P.s and candidates the following extract from a letter from Lord Rothermere: 'I cannot make it too abundantly clear that under no circumstances whatsoever will I support Mr. Baldwin unless I know exactly what his policy is going to be, unless I have complete guarantees that such policy will be carried out if his Party achieves office, and unless I am acquainted with the names of at least eight or ten of his most prominent colleagues in the next Ministry.'

Baldwin set aside the letter and remarked, 'A more preposterous and insolent demand was never made on the leader of any political party. I repudiate it with contempt and I will fight that attempt at domination to the end.' The audience rose and cheered him. Both parties in Parliament did the same that afternoon. Baldwin's popularity in the party was largely restored.

It was complete victory for him, and Lord Rothermere's lack of political judgement had thrown his ally, Beaverbrook, at Baldwin's feet.

But Beaverbrook was soon up again. Four days later he said, 'I will never falter until Empire Free Trade is the adopted policy of this country. And if the Conservative Party will not have Empire Free Trade now and here and without me, if it pleases the leaders, then the country must have it with me, but without those Conservative leaders.'

At that time Neville Chamberlain, though a personal friend of Baldwin, was eager to come to terms with Beaverbrook. He knew that the feelings against Baldwin's leadership inside the Tory Party were both real and dangerous. Loyalty to his political chief halted him from any action against Baldwin, though he must have understood that had Baldwin resigned the leadership (which he nearly did), he himself would almost certainly have been his successor.

Instead Chamberlain helped Baldwin to win a vote of confidence at a party meeting by 462 votes to 116.

Another by-election was now fought at St. George's, Westminster. Duff Cooper was Baldwin's man. An Independent was attacking him, supported by the full weight of the Beaverbrook and Rothermere newspapers. Baldwin went along to the Queen's Hall on 18 March 1931 and made the 'Harlot' speech. He referred to 'power without responsibility, the prerogative of the harlot through the ages'. It was damaging but, as will later be recorded, Baldwin was not the man who thought of it.

Duff Cooper won the St. George's by-election.

But the danger of division in the Conservative ranks had been deadly. Within ten days a truce between the parties was publicly proclaimed. Neville Chamberlain was sent to 'ask Lord Beaverbrook his terms of support'.

An agreement was reached at Stornoway House.

In his book, *Friends*, Beaverbrook gives the following account of it (p. 65):

'Throughout the winter and spring of 1931 the Tory Party was disrupted by disputes. Empire Free Traders and the Tory Free Food diehards were attacking each other with fury.

'By mid-summer Baldwin was under such pressure that he had to give way to the Empire Free Traders who were called also Empire Crusaders.

'He accepted our policy in a written treaty of peace signed at Stornoway House. Of course, he did not intend to carry out this bargain. He had deceived before and I knew he would do it again. But Chamberlain signed the document and I was convinced he could be trusted. He would compel Baldwin to keep his promise—or so I believed.'

Meanwhile, unknown to Beaverbrook, Chamberlain was reporting to a secret meeting of the Tory Shadow Cabinet that Beaverbrook was 'chastened by defeat'. He added that he was under no illusion that war might not break out again, as 'Max is very like Gandhi'.

Baldwin made peace with Beaverbrook because he had to do it. The pressures on him to resign from Tory leadership were so strong that on 1 March 1931 Chamberlain told Hoare that Baldwin had gone. An editorial was set up in *The Times* headed 'Mr. Baldwin withdraws'. It had to be destroyed when Baldwin decided he was indestructible.

After 1931 Beaverbrook never met Baldwin again. He saw him now and again in the park. But when he saw him, he always turned away and walked up another path.

8

TROUBLE IN PARADISE

Beaverbrook the Friend

WHEN the National Government was formed in 1931, with MacDonald as Prime Minister and with Baldwin in control, Beaverbrook hoped the Stornoway House Agreement would lead to Imperial Preference.

Instead the policy of the Ottawa Agreement emerged. Baldwin claimed later that the Ottawa Agreement satisfied the written bargain with Beaverbrook. The records clearly show that is not true. The Ottawa Agreement gave but a slice of the loaf that had been pledged at Stornoway House.

At Ottawa, Beaverbrook might have achieved his life-long aim of Imperial Preference, leading to Empire Free Trade. It was not to be. And it is an irony and a paradox that, apart from the opposition of men like Baldwin, the prize was snatched from his grasp by a temporary breach in his oldest friendship. That breach was caused in part by an act of suppression of news in the Canadian Press.

It happened like this. Beaverbrook's friendship with Bennett of Canada endured through the years. As early as 1912 Bennett had come from Canada to speak in Beaverbrook's constituency. He said there that the great policy should be 'to bring about the union of those nations [the Dominions] with the land they called and delighted to speak of as Mother'.

War came. Bennett and Bonar Law, Beaverbrook's closest friends, increased their influence and power in different parts of the Empire. Then, in October 1917, Bennett was disappointed because he was not included in the reshuffled Conservative Government in Canada, led by Sir Robert Borden, the Conservative Prime Minister. Bennett wrote to Aitken suggesting that he might come over to England and stand as a supporter of Lloyd George's Coalition Government in the British House of Commons. He felt convinced that Borden had cheated him by promising him a Senatorship and then running out on his promise.

Aitken, as we have seen, became Lord Beaverbrook. But Bennett was spared from a seat in the Senate which would have curtailed his own political advancement and might have prevented him becoming the Prime Minister of his country. In a fit of depression on 22 December 1917 Bennett wrote, 'He would be a bold man who would venture to say that even twenty-five years from now Canada would not be part of the United States'.

By the end of 1927 Bennett had been elected leader of the Conservative Party in Canada.

At the close of the year 1929 Bennett came to England. Beaverbrook was in the midst of his campaign for Empire Free Trade. Bennett was enormously impressed with the prospects of this campaign for Imperial Preference. On 4 December, on the boat going back to Canada, he wrote to Lord Beaverbrook, 'I have never left G.B. since you went there to live with greater pride in you and your work. I have seen you as a businessman, author, soldier, journalist, but it was all a bit futile. Now you are at a real job which may embrace all the others, but it means so much to the world that I am certain, in the end, although the *Express* may be in your mind now, you will think of the Empire and what you can do for it. It is your great opportunity. You are making rapid progress. It well may be that this great campaign will take you very, very far, even to the highest position in politics. That is not what I am thinking of. You are now giving your best for a cause: not money, position or circulation. These well may come, but this is the real Max at his best: the son of his father—the Scots-Canadian giving of his best that the old Mother may gather her children about her and continue to be what she has so long been and what she has nearly been no more, "the Mother of the Free".'

In a Press interview before Christmas, Bennett told the newspapers, 'There is greater interest in Empire trade in Britain today even than in the time of Chamberlain. As for those who criticize Lord Beaverbrook and refer to the Empire crusade as "stunt", I have to say that as long ago as eighteen years, Beaverbrook wrote to me suggesting that I should devote myself to Empire trade development.' By mid-summer of 1930 Bennett was attacking Mackenzie King's Liberal Government at a General Election in Canada. He said, 'I am for the British Empire next to Canada, the only difference being that some gentlemen [Mackenzie King and his Ministers] are for the United States before Canada. I am for the British Empire after Canada.'

Bennett won that election and became Prime Minister of Canada. Across the Atlantic, Beaverbrook flung up his hat with joy. His telegram of congratulation was ecstatic. It remained unanswered. At this hour, when every dream might have come true, a nightmare of division befell the two friends. It arose from an interview Beaverbrook had given to the *Toronto Globe* in May 1930. In it he praised the Liberal budget of Mackenzie King which had granted improved tariff preference to Britain. The *Globe* suppressed the interview until the last hours before the polling of the General Election in Canada, then printed Beaverbrook's words, uttered many weeks earlier, as if he was coming out at that moment against Bennett and in support of Mackenzie King. It was a dirty bit of journalism. It outraged Bennett. He felt he had been betrayed by his friend. Two months later Bennett arrived in England for an Imperial conference.

He made no sign to Beaverbrook. He sent no word. Instead,

he put forward proposals for another system of tariffs, and added, 'In our opinion, Empire Free Trade is neither desirable nor possible, for it would defeat the very purpose we are striving to achieve. All that is helpful in Empire Free Trade may be secured by Empire preferences. All that is harmful may in this way be avoided.'

Beaverbrook wrote three letters to his old friend. Bennett answered none of them. In the first letter Beaverbrook asked for a meeting. In the second letter, in more formal phrases, he said, 'If we in England refuse to assume the hegemony of the Empire, why not consider taking it for Canada?' Bennett read and discussed this letter with his colleagues. But no written response came.

Four days afterwards Bennett called Beaverbrook on the telephone and said loudly, 'I suppose my picture is turned to the wall?' Beaverbrook repeated his apologies and explanations, but Bennett was unmovable.

In his third letter Beaverbrook said, 'I have never consciously done you any injury. Inadvertently, I may have been the cause of much damage. I can do nothing to put that wrong right again. But my punishment would be too heavy if an affection of a lifetime ended in coldness and detachment. Bonar Law said to Asquith when the first Coalition Government fell, "If a man does an injury to another for which there is no redress, then there can be no explanations". It may be that protestations are futile in my present predicament. If so, it will be a grief and sorrow for the rest of my days. But I would not willingly try to reconstruct the broken bridge if the traffic is not passing to and fro.' Bennett made no reply.

It was a moment when the battle between Baldwin and Beaverbrook had come to a crunch. Baldwin called a Party meeting at the Caxton Hall on the very day that South Paddington, a by-election where a Beaverbrook candidate named Admiral Taylor was fighting against Baldwin's Conservative nominee, went to the polls. At the Caxton Hall,

Baldwin said that seventeen members of his Party in the House of Commons had sent a demand for his resignation. He said he must get a complete vote of confidence from the Party or resign. The audience called for Beaverbrook. Beaverbrook arose and tried to speak. Baldwin's supporters howled him down. The voting at the Caxton Hall was 462 for Baldwin and 116 against him. On the other hand, South Paddington that evening returned Beaverbrook's Empire Free Trade candidate with a good majority.

And that very night, unexpectedly, Bennett came knocking at the door of Stornoway House, without previous notice, to visit his old friend.

Beaverbrook sums up the day and the damage to the cause of Empire in the following words: 'If I had not lost Bennett's collaboration at the critical period of our campaign in Britain, our Empire Free Trade plan under his influence might have been forced upon the Tory Party during the autumn of 1930 while the Imperial conference was in session. The fault was mine. Without doubt I should have given real assistance to Bennett's electoral campaign in Canada. And Bennett should have been moved by my explanations. But he was not free from rancour. Political issues often turn on personal disputes. It was a pity and I must take the blame.'

At this time Bennett had turned sixty. Beaverbrook was over fifty years of age. The British General Election took place in October 1931. By then Baldwin had come under such pressure that he had once more shifted and accepted the written treaty of peace with Beaverbrook, signed at Stornoway House and known as the Stornoway House Agreement.

The National Government came to power in October 1931, with the Socialist Ramsay MacDonald as Prime Minister, but with the Conservative Baldwin the real master of the House. Immediately the issue of the Empire and Imperial Preference came to the forefront of affairs on both sides of the Atlantic.

In the New Year of 1932 the British Chancellor of the

Exchequer introduced a Bill which would have put a 10 per cent duty against Empire and foreigner alike (excluding, of course, wheat, meat, and other raw materials). Bennett cabled Beaverbrook saying that such a tax would create an atmosphere that would make the success of the Imperial conference, fixed to take place in Ottawa in July, well-nigh impossible.

Neville Chamberlain, whom Beaverbrook trusted, was approached, and announced on 4 February in Parliament, 'On Dominion goods we will impose no duties until after Ottawa'. On 5 February Bennett telegraphed his congratulations.

In mid-July the Imperial conference began in Ottawa. In spite of the fact that the British delegation was led by Baldwin, who was opposed to all and every tax on foreign food, Neville Chamberlain, the son and successor of Joseph Chamberlain, was a leading member of the British party. Bruce of Australia had always been a supporter of Empire Free Trade and Bennett was taking the chair.

The two friends, Bennett and Beaverbrook, seemed to be within grasping point of their life-long hope and dream.

But Bennett and Chamberlain disliked each other. They could not agree. They scratched and scowled. They allowed themselves to be separated by minor matters and so lost the major engagement.

Beaverbrook was not invited to Ottawa. He said of this, 'My mistakes were many, my miscalculations and indiscretions were damaging. . . . I behaved very foolishly sometimes and quite badly often. Possibly my greatest blunder was my failure to support Bennett in his election campaign of 1930, considering my ample resources. Perhaps it was due to the memory of my default and failure that Bennett did not ask me to Ottawa during the conference. How I longed for such an invitation. How I regretted my exclusion from personal contact with him in the crisis of the negotiations. Had I been given the opportunity to see Bennett every day during the conference, in the words of his own favourite quotation, it might have been "something attempted, something done". It has been said of me, and rightly, "The cause was great, greater than the man".'

By August the Ottawa conference was done, and done for good. The British delegation had fallen out amongst each other over a duty on foreign meat. Baldwin, who, under the fear of losing his grip of the Conservative Party, had agreed to Imperial Preference on the Stornoway House Treaty, was glad of an excuse to renegue. He always felt it wrong to tax foreign food. He declared with gladness, 'Chamberlain said he could not oppose it [a demand by Australia for a duty on foreign meat] and remain in the Government. Runciman could not support it and remain in the Government.' Baldwin asked J. H. Thomas, a Socialist who had left his own party to join the National Government, whether he would submit the dispute in the British delegation over food taxes to Prime Minister Ramsay MacDonald back in England. Thomas, who before he joined the MacDonald–Baldwin National Government had denounced in the British Parliament the Bennett Empire plan as 'humbug', replied to Baldwin, 'I'll put it to Ramsay and I'll tell him a lie. I'll tell him I am for the meat duty—which I am not—and that will settle it.' He meant that MacDonald would oppose anything he believed he, Thomas, was for. Baldwin's comment was, 'In the event the fight was settled without a duty, but it was very decent of Jim [to tell a lie]'.

On 15 August 1932 Neville Chamberlain wrote in his diary, 'Another black day. Saw Bruce [leader of the Australian delegation] and Gullett [Australian Minister of State for Trade and Customs] with Hailsham and told them that we could not give them a duty [on foreign meat].' That day marked the death of Joseph Chamberlain's grand design. The Ottawa conference slid into a pit of petty bargaining and horse-trading.

Baldwin came home. In private and in public he blamed Bennett for the failure of the conference. He said, 'Bennett had a brain storm every day which wiped out what he had agreed to the day before'. He quoted with approval a former Liberal

Minister's description of Bennett: 'He has the manners of a Chicago policeman and the temperament of a Hollywood film star.'

It is true to say that until the day he died Bennett never lost the weight of grief over his failure at Ottawa to achieve the economic unity of the British Empire. Years later, at the time of Munich, Chamberlain demonstrated to the world that he was a man who preferred to negotiate alone. But he met in Bennett a man with a like view of life. He looked upon his Cabinet colleagues as something less than himself in ability and responsibility. The story was told of him sitting alone in his club muttering to himself. A stranger asked, 'What is he doing? What is he saying?' The answer was, 'He's holding a Cabinet meeting'.

At Ottawa, Bennett and Chamberlain quarrelled so deeply that their breach was never healed. Chamberlain spoke of Bennett's aggressive tones and complained that he concealed essential facts. He complained of Bennett's half-heartedness in putting into practice the high Imperial sentiments which he preached. The effect on Chamberlain was to alter for ever his views on the Empire. When he went to Ottawa, he had the vision of Joseph Chamberlain in his heart. When he came away, that picture of the Empire had faded.

While this Ottawa conference failed in its main aims, an economic hurricane was sweeping across the world. It struck Canada with devastation. In eighteen months from the time Bennett became Prime Minister until the time the conference was held, the price of wheat fell more than 50 per cent a bushel. Farmers were ruined. Hunger stalked the land.

Bennett, in the eyes of his contemporaries, bore the blame. Beaverbrook later publicly declared that when the secret records of those months are revealed, Bennett will stand before the light of history as a leader of wisdom, courage, and faith.

Beaverbrook had possession of the Bennett papers, which are not to be published until 1967. He said, 'When all the facts are told, the name of Richard Bedford Bennett, Prime Minister, will be exalted. His picture should be adorning the boardrooms of railways, banks and insurance companies throughout the Dominion.'

On 14 October 1935 Bennett went down to defeat in Canada. He wrote to Beaverbrook and came to live the last years of his life at Juniper Hill, Mickleham Down, close to Cherkley. At the time of the Ottawa conference he had been asked by J. H. Thomas what he wanted. Thomas said the King would ask him this question as soon as he got home to London. Bennett said that he did not want a peerage yet. But Baldwin agreed that when the time came, Bennett should enter the House of Lords. However, when Bennett made his home in England after retiring from the Premiership in Canada, Chamberlain, then Prime Minister, so lingered in the dislike which he had formed for Bennett at Ottawa that he refused to recommend him for the House of Lords. It was not until Churchill became Prime Minister after war broke out that Bennett was made a Viscount.

To the end of his life Bennett retained the habits that had helped to form his character. He read a chapter of the Bible every day of his life. He would do no work on Sundays though he could not resist answering the telephone at all hours of the day. In his closing years he agreed that to see a film on Sunday night would not contradict his Sabbatarian principles.

He used to come to lunch on a Sunday with Beaverbrook. A life-long teetotaller, he would nevertheless drink more than one glass of *crème de menthe*. He did so because Beaverbrook told him that it was a teetotaller's drink. When asked whether Bennett believed there was no alcohol in *crème de menthe*, Beaverbrook shook his head and said, 'He was happy if he was told it was a teetotaller's drink'. Bennett would also take sherry in the soup, declaring that the heat of the soup burned out the alcohol in the sherry. He served good wine at table. And the wine was good because his friend Beaverbrook gave him advice on its purchase and also gave him wine from his cellar.

He suffered from diabetes. This made it necessary for him to have an injection every day. His doctor told him that he could train one of the staff to give Bennett this injection. Bennett replied, 'How much would it cost if you gave me the injection each day?' The doctor replied, 'A pound a day'. Bennett said, 'Oh, £365 a year, except Leap Year. That's not too bad.' So every morning at 8 o'clock the doctor arrived at Bennett's house to give him his injection as he lay in his bath. If the doctor arrived even a minute or two after 8, he was scolded. On Sundays the time of arrival was postponed until 8.45.

Bennett had three great topics of conversation. The first was his intimate friendship with King George V. The second was Max Beaverbrook. The third was Guildford Cathedral and how he, a life-long Methodist, had helped to finance an Episcopalian building. Each morning he would dress himself in a hammertail coat and, carrying a silk hat and knobbed cane, would come to the door to bid farewell to the doctor.

Though he might often have wed, he never did so. He heeded not the wisdom of Benjamin Franklin, who declared, 'He that has not yet a wife, is not yet a complete man'. At the same time, a woman who married him would have had an interesting but difficult path to go. He was devoted to his sister, Mildred. When she died, he sat himself alone in a room for hours reading the Scriptures aloud. But once when she asked him for 250 dollars to buy 'something or other', Bennett let out a roar and gave her hell, so that she burst into tears. On another occasion, during the days of prohibition, Bennett found his sister sharing a bottle of champagne with an old friend. Bennett declared that both his sister and her friend were drunk and refused to say one word more to her for two days.

Though he referred to *crème de menthe* as a 'soft drink', he used to denounce drink and drunkenness to the end of his days with heat and ability. He thought that 'Drink the Demon' was responsible for the ruin of family life and the despair of harmless people. He would provide others with drink and with cigars or cigarettes, but, for himself, he stood apart from those things.

Towards the end of his days he wrote to his friend Max Beaverbrook. He said in that letter, 'God bless you and keep you and give you health and strength to continue your unrivalled service to our Empire. The British people throughout the world are grateful for all you have done and are doing, but not one in those millions has greater pride in your success, or holds you in more affectionate regard than your friend of boyhood days who still subscribes himself ever yours, faithfully, devotedly and affectionately, Dick.'

At about this same time, Beaverbrook wrote to Bennett, ending his letter, 'All my life I have been your disciple, following in your footsteps and fortunate in your guidance. Yours ever, Max.'

Beaverbrook's hopes of the Empire were never quenched. Many years ago (14 November 1927), he wrote to his friend Bennett, 'The centre of the Empire is passing westwards. It will take years to pass from England to Canada. But in the long run the transference will be effected, for in the course of time the development of the vast natural resources of Canada must give it the acknowledged right to play the leading part.' It might seem a far dream. But Beaverbrook always believed it could come true.

About the Common Market, he was convinced that there could be no economic unity without political unity.

He foresaw a time when Britain could become to Europe what the State of Rhode Island is to the United States of America—respected, proud, but insignificant when the great issues of war, peace, and the social and economic conditions of a nation are settled.

He also was a Scot. Some Scots are bred to the belief that in national affairs 'the greater draws the less'. They believe that since their marriage with the English, the English bridegroom has had the big share of the joint, while the Scottish bride in the north labours to prepare it. Some Scots have the instinct that if Britain enters Europe, the great mass of the Continental lands will draw the lesser Islanders into their control and sway. Beaverbrook was such a Scot.

Baldwin charged Beaverbrook with wanting power. It was a just charge. He once said, 'Mr. Baldwin has the power. I haven't. I wish I had.' Beaverbrook wanted power to bring about policies in which he believed. If others would not do it, then he would.

He made his position clear years before when he spoke to Bonar Law. Bonar Law pressed him strongly to abandon Fleet Street and go back to politics. Bonar Law felt that this was the best way to win Imperial Preference. Or, if Beaverbrook continued in Fleet Street, Bonar Law urged him to work subserviently with the official Conservative Party and support its programme without qualification. Beaverbrook replied, 'No. In politics I am bound—for no man can really be a politician without submitting to the necessary trammels of Party. In the Press, on the contrary, I am free and can work from outside. And my belief is that parties in this country can only be induced to support the Imperial cause by external influences, like the pressure of popular opinion. Inside the Conservative Party, whether as politician or journalist, I should be prohibited from appealing to popular opinion against the decision of my leaders.'

9
WAR AND AWARENESS

Beaverbrook the Peacemaker

BETWEEN 1932 and 1939, war or peace became a main theme of men's consideration. Beaverbrook was a man of peace. The record shows it.

He believed in holding out the hand of friendship while carrying a big stick in the other hand. He always believed in peace from strength, not weakness.

'Scholarships not battleships' was the cry of the Left when Hitler's jackboots were making Europe shudder. It meant that most sane people would prefer spending money on schools than on ships.

But it would be as sensible to yell 'Pensions not police' at a time when the crime-wave was rising.

The modern Labour Party believes in the need for arms. But in the inter-war years they described war-loans as 'borrowing for death'. Four months—just four months—before Hitler invaded Poland, the Labour Party opposed conscription because it would 'weaken and divide the country'. This party also had refused to support a campaign to recruit volunteers for the armed forces. (The Labour Party were in good company over conscription. Winston Churchill opposed it almost up to the outbreak of the 1939 war.)

In 1938, Sir Archibald Sinclair, leader of the Liberal Party, said it would be 'a disastrous blunder for Britain to organize an army for operations on the Continent'. In 1939, the year war began, he too opposed conscription.

But the men who must bear the brunt of the blame for Britain's unpreparedness in entering war were those in charge of our national affairs. The Labour Party from 1923 to 1945 held only three years of power.

From 1923 until 1937, the men who held the top place of power and of responsibility in Britain were Baldwin, Ramsay MacDonald, Baldwin, MacDonald, MacDonald–Baldwin, Baldwin–MacDonald, Baldwin. During eleven of those fourteen years Baldwin was, as Conservative leader, in control of the majority in the House of Commons. During that time Beaverbrook fought to build more planes, to grow more food, to modernize and equip the Army and Navy.

On 23 November 1932 Churchill for the first time in Parliament warned the nation of the unleashed menace in Germany. Baldwin, at that time, and in the coming years, chose ignorance as his protection against action. He declared later that he did not realize fully what was happening. He was a man who was happy for 'experts' to understand the difficult problems. ' "Consult and trust the man on the spot", said Baldwin—but did not.'[1] Baldwin said in Parliament in 1932, 'This is a question for the young men rather than the old men. When the next war comes and European civilization is wiped out, as it will be . . . then do not let them lay the blame on the old men. Let them remember that they principally and they alone are responsible for the terror that has fallen on the earth.' (But the old men, not the young, held the reins of power in Britain.)

The next Air Estimates introduced were £340,000 less than the year before and £1,000,000 less than the estimates of the last year of the 1929–31 Labour Government.

On 8 March 1934 Baldwin gave this undertaking in Parliament to Churchill: 'This Government will see to it that in air strength and air power this country shall no longer be in a

[1]Vansittart, *The Mist Procession*, page 352.

position inferior to any country within striking distance of our shores.'

On 28 November 1934, in the House of Commons, he said: 'His Majesty's Government are determined in no conditions to accept any position of inferiority with regard to what air force may be raised in Germany in the future.'

Churchill stated:

1. Germany had an illegal air force.

2. Within three years that air force would be twice as strong as our own.

Baldwin denied it. He said, 'It is not the case that Germany is rapidly approaching equality with us. Her real strength is not 50 per cent of our strength in Europe today.'

In later years Baldwin blamed Beaverbrook for attacking him over his policies and blamed the Foreign Office for a failure to give him the facts about German rearmament.

The charge against the Foreign Office is untrue. There was a man working in Hitler's Air Ministry who risked his life to supply one of the top men in the British Civil Service with accurate figures of Germany's growing air strength. These figures were passed on to the Foreign Office. Baldwin said, 'Neither I nor any advisers from whom we could get accurate information had any idea of the exact rate at which production could be, and admittedly was being, speeded up in Germany. We could get no facts.' The facts were there. Vansittart in his account of these days observes, 'If S.B. had no facts, he was the rasher to say we had a 50 per cent margin [over Germany]'.

In March 1935 Hitler publicly declared that Germany's air strength was equal to that of Britain. Baldwin said he did not believe it. (Records now show that Germany was already out-building Britain in the air.)

Baldwin said, 'That responsibility is the responsibility of the Government as a whole, and we are all responsible and we are all to blame'. He told his supporters at an Albert Hall meeting, 'No Government in this country could live a day, that was content to have an Air Force of any inferiority to any country within striking distance of our shores'.

In 1935 an election was fought. Many of the electors still believed in the prospects of Peace and opposed rearmament. Shortly before polling day, on 31 October 1935, Baldwin said, 'Do not fear or misunderstand when the Government say they are looking to our defences. I give you my word there will be no great armaments.'

One year later, 12 November 1936, he told the House of Commons he would speak with 'appalling candour'. He said, 'From 1933 I myself and my friends were all getting very worried about what was happening in Europe. I asked myself what chance was there of this country, where the feeling expressed at Fulham[1] was so common, being so changed in the next year or two that the country will give a mandate for rearmament? Now supposing I had gone to the country [last year] and had said, "Germany is rearming. We must rearm." Does anyone think this pacifist democracy would have rallied to that cry? Not at that moment. I cannot think of any change which would have made the loss of the election, from my point of view, more certain. We won the election with a large majority.' Baldwin's official biographer, G. M. Young, says of this speech: 'Never has a statesman done so much damage to his own good name.'

If words mean anything, those words meant that Baldwin had sold the electors short of truth in order to make a profit at the polls.

But if Baldwin won one election by this means, he certainly helped to lose the next in 1945. Baldwin retired from the Premiership in 1937. By 1945 men had died on the beaches of Dunkirk, in the cold waters of the Norwegian fjords, in the hot and sullen waters of the Orient because of the lack of pre-war

[1] Fulham was a by-election where a 'scholarships not battleships' peace candidate won a surprise victory over the Hon. William Astor, now Lord Astor.

preparedness. The fighting men and their families did not forget the pre-war years of Tory rule, when it came to the 1945 election. They were sick for a change in Government. They admired Churchill. They liked Churchill. They owed their freedom to Churchill. But the British public is not in the habit of handing out any bonus for services rendered. They remembered the pre-war Baldwin–Chamberlain era of Tory rule. They voted Labour into power.

In March 1936 Hitler broke the Locarno Treaty and marched his troops into the Rhineland. The German generals in command were told that if they met opposition, they were to retire at once into Germany. France wished to kick Hitler out of the Rhineland. They were told by Britain that they would do it at their peril and without support from this country. So they did nothing but protest.

A few days later Baldwin announced the appointment of Sir Thomas Inskip as the man to take charge of our Defence. The nation at that time expected and wanted Churchill to get the job. Baldwin knew Churchill would do something Hitler would not like and kept him out.

Churchill, when told of Inskip's appointment in the Lobby of the House of Commons, remarked, 'It is a clerical error'. In the smoking-room he said, 'There has been no such monstrous appointment since the Roman Emperor Caligula made his horse a consul'.

It was Inskip's first Cabinet post. He was a sincere man with a faith in God. But faith in God does not by itself equip somebody to match a Hitler in preparing a nation for war. Inskip's enemies called him a 'bum-faced puritan'. He said of himself, 'It never occurred to me that I was likely to be asked to accept these responsibilities. Nor did it ever occur to me—I can say this in all seriousness—that I would ever be able to discharge these duties even if they were offered to me.' It is fair to say that this assessment of himself, in the light of history, seems right.

Inskip was surprised to be given the job of Minister of

Co-ordination of Defence because it had been promised by Baldwin privately but definitely to another man—Sir Samuel Hoare.

Beaverbrook charged Baldwin with dishonesty. He said he was a man not to be trusted. The public continued to trust Baldwin until war came. But in view of this charge of fickleness and instability, it is worth examining how Hoare was robbed of his inheritance.

Soon after the 1935 election, Mussolini began to menace Abyssinia. Baldwin did not like foreign policy or foreigners. They bored him. He was deeply interested in home affairs, but he would take Foreign Office papers back to Chequers or Downing Street, and leave them unread, while in bed he scanned the detective stories that he kept around him.

Hoare was in charge of the Foreign Office. He was due to make a speech at the League of Nations in Geneva. It was a tough speech, threatening Mussolini. He showed the draft to Baldwin, who commented, 'That's all right. It must have taken you a long time to make it up.' The whole British Cabinet agreed to Hoare's strong words.

Hoare made his speech. It was hailed as a triumph. Nevertheless, on 3 October 1935, Mussolini, informed by Laval, the French Foreign Minister, that France would not go to war, marched into Abyssinia. The League of Nations, in applying sanctions against Italy, hesitated to include denying oil and closing the Suez Canal, lest this might lead to war.

In December, Hoare, on his way to Switzerland for a holiday, saw Laval in Paris. He had been told by Baldwin to do a deal with Laval if he could, and to settle the Abyssinian matter without war. Hoare got the best terms he could from Laval, who was in touch by telephone with Mussolini during the interview. It was appeasement. It was agreed to give part of Abyssinia to Mussolini.

Baldwin and the whole British Cabinet knew the terms and agreed to the proposition. Hoare went on his way to Switzerland. The French Foreign Office, pledged to secrecy, leaked the whole plan to the French Press. The well-known writer Pertinax published it in full.

A storm arose against the plan in Britain and elsewhere. Baldwin spoke on the phone to Hoare in Switzerland and told him, 'Don't worry. I have complete control of the situation. Stay where you are.' Hoare stayed.

Baldwin spoke strongly in favour of the Hoare–Laval plan in the House of Commons. He said, 'My lips are not yet unsealed. Were the trouble over, I could make my case, and I guarantee not a man would go into the lobby against me.' Eden on that same day told an audience that Hoare and Laval were acting in the framework of the League of Nations and at their request. Indeed, the whole plan had been prepared with the knowledge and consent of the inner circle of the League.

Hoare had by now returned to London. But public clamour against the plan continued. The chins of Baldwin and his Cabinet colleagues began to wobble and their knees to knock. They decided to climb down.

Hoare asked Beaverbrook to come to his house and see him. They were joined there by Vansittart, Permanent Under-Secretary for Foreign Affairs, who was the real architect of the Hoare–Laval proposals. His was the heart, hand, and head in the centre of it all.

Hoare was strongly in favour of defying the clamour and pursuing the plan. He decided to resign in protest against Baldwin's surrender. Vansittart said he would resign too. Beaverbrook dissuaded him. In *The Mist Procession* (page 542), Vansittart grudgingly and after much abuse of Beaverbrook says, 'It might be more dignified to go first, but my leanings towards resignation were corrected—curiously enough—by Beaverbrook, who pointed out that there would soon be no public services if public servants resigned on issues of policy'. (Vansittart was close indeed to Baldwin, and in fact never said a word in criticism of the Tory leader until Baldwin's power was lost.)

Chamberlain came to see Hoare on Baldwin's behalf and returned to Baldwin with the tale of Hoare's defiance. Then he came back again with Baldwin's benediction and a message: 'Resign now. We will abandon the plan—but we will not abandon you. Do not attack the Government. And we'll have you back in it again soon.' The promise was that Sir Samuel's flight from Paradise would be brief. But Paradise, as Satan found, is often easier to leave than to re-enter.

Hoare put all this before Beaverbrook. Beaverbrook, who wanted to pull Baldwin down, nevertheless said, 'Accept'. He was a party to what politicians call a deal and others call a swindle.

Hoare, of course, was wrong to resign. He should have defied Baldwin and told the nation the facts. But he listened to the voice of his own ambition and to appeals 'not to damage the Party'. On 19 December he made his speech of resignation in the House of Commons. His speech was not damaging to Baldwin.

Sir Austen Chamberlain spoke in defence of Baldwin and the Government. Sir Austen was not beloved by Baldwin. He had often been a critic. Baldwin had helped Bonar Law to turn him out of the leadership of the Tory Party. Once at dinner, when word came to Baldwin that Sir Austen had been criticizing him, Baldwin remarked, 'Austen has driven another nail in his coffin today'. Then, rubbing his stomach with glee, he said, 'I do love strawberries and cream'.

But on this occasion of the Hoare–Laval debate, Baldwin had promised Austen Chamberlain that if he would speak for the Government, he would succeed Sir Samuel Hoare as Foreign Secretary. In the House of Commons debate, Sir Austen spoke out strongly on Baldwin's behalf. Baldwin carried the day. He then appointed Anthony Eden, not Austen Chamberlain, as Foreign Secretary.

Now came some of Beaverbrook's mischief. Instead of following Hoare's soft line, of which he had approved,

Beaverbrook began to scream that Baldwin was a betrayer, that he had gone out on a limb with Baldwin in support of the deal over Abyssinia, and that Baldwin had retreated. 'He sawed off the limb and I am badly bruised because he deserted me.' That was Beaverbrook's lament. It was a dishonest lament, for he had known all along of Hoare's attitude and encouraged him to come to terms with Baldwin.

It is fair to say that neither Baldwin nor Beaverbrook gain great glory from these events. But they are examples of the cunning of the contest and the slippery mischief of it all.

Post-war documents show that had the Hoare–Laval pact gone through, Mussolini was ready to end his attack on Abyssinia and to separate himself from Hitler. He always took an interest in British affairs.

Once, in Rome, he asked Beaverbrook about the British Socialists. The Italian dictator was convinced they would soon be running Britain.

Beaverbrook spoke of Cripps. Mussolini asked if he had money. Beaverbrook spoke of the fortune of Lady Cripps and explained that it came from Eno's Fruit Salts. Mussolini roared with laughter. He said, 'In Italy we use castor oil'.

The time now came when Hoare expected to be taken back into Baldwin's arms. He let it be known that he expected Baldwin to pay the debt. He hinted in the Press and told his friends in political circles that he would soon have to make speeches hostile to Baldwin if something were not offered him.

In June 1936 Baldwin offered Hoare the job of Minister for Co-ordination of Defence. Neville Chamberlain suggested, on Baldwin's behalf, that Hoare should speak in a Defence debate. Hoare spoke on the lines Chamberlain had suggested.

Next morning, *The Times* denounced Hoare's speech as a clumsy bid for office. Baldwin ran out on Hoare. He gave the job to Inskip.

At that time Geoffrey Dawson was Editor of *The Times*. He had a strong influence on Baldwin. Vansittart writes (*The*

Mist Procession, page 364), 'Northcliffe had said Dawson "is just naturally pro-German. He can't help it." '

Baldwin relied on Dawson. He said to him, 'It is easier for me to talk these matters over with you than with any of my political colleagues'. It was in June 1936 that, with Dawson backing him and without the knowledge of many of his colleagues, Baldwin was in favour of a secret meeting with Hitler. He hoped to take Eden to Berlin with him to meet the Führer. The idea was discussed with Hitler (Tom Jones's. *A Diary with Letters*, pages 201 and 218 and elsewhere). Tom Jones says of his own interview with Hitler, 'I pointed out that Mr. Baldwin was a shy and modest statesman who had never entirely got over his astonishment at finding himself Prime Minister. . . . The Führer smiled and interjected, "And I also". '

Hitler sent the British Tory leader a gift.

Tom Jones at this time, after a week-end at Chequers (23 May 1936, *Diary*, page 209), commented, 'Hitler feels quite unequal to standing up alone to Russia and is disturbed by the way Russia and Czechoslovakia are concocting an air policy. He is therefore asking for an alliance with us to form a bulwark against the spread of Communism. Our Prime Minister [Baldwin] is not indisposed to attempt this.'

But Eden opposed such schemes. So did the British public. And nothing came of it all.

Some years later, in 1941, Baldwin told me his own views of those troubled times. Of the 'sealed lips' speech he said, 'It was a silly thing to say. It was the silliest thing I ever said. But what could we do? We were in a hole. Sam Hoare was tired. The very last thing he said to us all and to Anthony [Eden] on the station platform as he left to see Laval in Paris was, "Don't worry about me. I won't commit us to anything." Next thing we heard through the Press leak in Paris was that Sam had done his deal. Now I have instincts about people and, whatever you say about me, my instincts are usually right. I felt instinctively that the man Laval was in the pay of Mussolini and his instrument. Events now seem to show I wasn't far wrong. We had information that France would not act with us. And that if orders were given to mobilize the French army, there would be revolution and rioting in France. Sealed lips was a silly thing to say. But the fact was there was nothing for me to say. We were in a hole.'

This statement does not explain why Baldwin and his Cabinet in truth backed the Hoare–Laval plan until the public turned against it. It also raises the question why, if the Prime Minister distrusted Laval so deeply, he ever allowed Hoare to see Laval. Or, if he did allow it, failed to give his Minister explicit instructions about the interview, but only told him to do a deal.

Baldwin seemed in the afterlight of events to blame Beaverbrook in some way for all this. He was lame from rheumatoid arthritis. He used a stick as a sort of punt-pole to aid his progress. But almost as soon as he opened his door to me, he said, 'You're the first man to be employed by the *Express* [I had left the *Express* some time before] who ever came inside my house—and you are likely to be the last. You can't be expected to write anything but the wrong sort of stuff if you work for Beaverbrook. He is a black Calvinist. He'll probably end up as a religious maniac.'

Baldwin liked to be thought the sort of man who always smells a newspaper before he reads it. He said to a friend of his about Pressmen visiting Downing Street, 'We have had this place swabbed out since I became Prime Minister and I am not going to have it infected again'.

Vansittart commented on this attitude, 'Since Beaverbrook and Rothermere were of all men the most outspoken in antipathy to Baldwin's causes, they and theirs were especially to be excluded. . . . He hated the Beaver above all other creatures—though the Beaver courted him between insults. . . . S.B. would have neither Lord . . . had not the Beaver seven houses and no home?' (*The Mist Procession*, pages 366, 367.)

Vansittart's verdict on Baldwin was 'the subtlest Celt that ever played the complete Englishman' (page 352). ' "You cannot serve God and Mammon"—but you can, and S.B. was thought once the man for the double task' (page 355).

The story of Baldwin came to a sorrowful close. He was haunted and harrowed by the hatred of the people who for so long held him in such high esteem. After the fall of France, he said, 'They hate me so'.

Baldwin's weakness was to pronounce and not to deliver. He gave neither material nor moral rearmament, though he promised both.

He heard of a former follower of his in Parliament who, when the railways and gates everywhere were being seized for scrap near the start of World War II, said, 'Let Lord Baldwin keep his gates at Apsley Hall. He needs them to protect him from the just indignation of the mob.'

It is interesting that Lord Beaverbrook was Minister of Supply at the time these gates were requisitioned.

Fences, railings, all manner of wrought iron was being torn away and taken for scrap. Beaverbrook requisitioned his own gates. He also requisitioned Baldwin's.

An appeal was made to Churchill, who said, 'Lay off Baldwin's gates'. So Baldwin's gates were saved.

Baldwin said to me last time I saw him, a lonely old man in the shadows, 'Time will prove me right. No man can be fairly judged till fifty years after he is dead. I was very popular after the Duke of Windsor left the country. When I and my wife drove along at the Coronation [of King George VI], I couldn't believe the people were cheering *me* like that. But they were. I said to my wife that it was roses now, but would be cabbages in a week or two. So it happened.'

Then, pointing to the view from the back of Apsley Hall, he said, 'Those hills are where Owen Glendower sat. The last place the Welsh occupied in England before we knocked them out. With a view like that to see every day, you don't worry much what people think of you.'

But Baldwin worried.

10

PROPAGANDA AND PROPHECY

Beaverbrook the Prophet

BEAVERBROOK failed to budge Baldwin and to get his policy of Empire adopted. On account of that, journals like the *New Statesman* have spread a theory about the *Daily Express* and the Beaverbrook newspapers. It may be called the 'Kiss of Death' philosophy. The suggestion is made that if Beaverbrook supported you, then you were bound to lose—or conversely that he was a false prophet, always picking the wrong side.

It is worth examining this charge to discover how much truth lies in it.

After Beaverbrook took control of the *Express* there were eleven General Elections in this country in his lifetime.

In the 1918 General Election, the so-called Khaki election, the *Express* was on the side of the angels. Lloyd George won.

In the 1922 election, after there had been trouble in Paradise and the Coalition had broken up, Beaverbrook backed Bonar Law. Bonar Law won.

In 1923, after Bonar Law's retirement, Baldwin went to the country on a programme which Beaverbrook opposed. Baldwin was defeated.

In 1924, the so-called 'Zinoviev letter' election, Beaverbrook supported Baldwin. Baldwin won.

In 1929, when Baldwin had abandoned any prospects of allegiance to Empire Free Trade and Imperial Preference, Beaverbrook did not support him. Baldwin lost the day.

So it can be seen that in the first five shots Beaverbrook hit the bull's-eye five times.

In 1931, after the formation of the National Government, Beaverbrook came out on the winning side; 1935, the same story.

In 1945, at the close of World War II, there was a débâcle for the Conservatives and Churchill. Labour swept to victory with a majority of 186. One cause of Churchill's defeat was a speech he broadcast to the nation in which he declared that if Labour won there would be some kind of Gestapo in this land. After the tumult and the shouting died, after the kings and captains of the Tory regiments had been unhorsed and rolled in the mud, blood, and dust of defeat, there was a meeting of all the defeated, as well as of the victorious, Conservative candidates. They spent the whole day doing little but abuse Beaverbrook for his responsibility in helping Churchill write and utter the Gestapo speech. The truth is that Beaverbrook played no part in preparing that oration. He wrote a letter to *The Times* in which he made this plain. Churchill has since confirmed it. Nevertheless, Beaverbrook and his newspapers supported the losing side in the electoral battle of 1945.

In 1950 the Tories won a moral victory. Churchill, having been sunk almost without trace in 1945, surfaced with all guns blazing. He came within a few votes of defeating the Socialists. Labour's majority was reduced to eight. All the same, Beaverbrook supported the Tory losers.

In 1951 Beaverbrook was on the winner. Churchill won a majority of sixteen and the Conservatives returned to power. 1955, another victory—this time with Eden and a majority of fifty-nine; 1959, the same story—with Macmillan in the saddle and a majority of 100.

So it can be said that in eleven elections since the year 1918, the *Daily Express* has been nine times on the winning side. Victory has perched nine times out of eleven upon their banners, while only twice have the banners been dragged in the dust of defeat. No other newspaper in the country can claim such a record.

In the course of the years, the *Express* has had other great victories. Its failure has been Empire Free Trade. Beaverbrook believed that the nation will weep about that failure yet.

Now it is said that the *Express* newspapers were wrong in predicting that there would be no war against Hitler. A phrase, 'There will be no war this year, or next year either', was hurled again and again at Beaverbrook like a ripe tomato or rotten egg by his enemies. From 19 September 1938, up till the very eve of the outbreak of war, on 14 August 1939, the *Daily Express* was predicting peace, not war. It is said that the *Express* in its support of Munich and its belief in the possibilities of peace, helped to soften the nation and encouraged its enemies in the belief that we would not fight. If this is so, then Beaverbrook and the *Express* are in good company.

Here are the names of a few of those who predicted peace: Mr. Neville Chamberlain, Prime Minister, and many of his Cabinet colleagues, including Sir Thomas Inskip, Defence Minister, and Mr. Hore-Belisha, Secretary of State for War; Mr. Clem Attlee, then Leader of the Opposition; Mr. Ernest Bevin, the Trade Union boss; Mr. Menzies of Australia; Mr. Litvinov of Russia; and of course Mr. Lloyd George and Mr. Winston Churchill. Both these last two were strong in predictions of peace. Both were among those who suffered from the illusion that Hitler might change. Mr. Lloyd George described Hitler as the 'George Washington of his country'. While in 1935, Mr. Winston Churchill said Hitler might 'go down in history as the man who restored honour and peace of mind to the great Germanic nation and brought it back serene, helpful and strong, to the forefront of the European family circle'.

Nowadays, three newspapers in Britain, the *Daily Express*, the *Sunday Express* and the *Evening Standard*, admit they supported Munich. So here I set out a list of some of the national newspapers *For* and *Against* Munich at the time of the agreement:

For	Against
Daily Express	*Reynolds News*
Sunday Express	
Evening Standard	
The Times	
Manchester Guardian	
Daily Mirror	
Daily Herald	
Daily Sketch	
Daily Mail	
Evening News	
The Star	
Sunday Times	
The Observer	
News-Chronicle	

The *Daily Worker* was against war with Hitler when Molotov and Ribbentrop signed their pact to divide Poland. It swerved into favour of war when Germany invaded Russia.

The *Manchester Guardian*, which has from time to time been critical of what it calls the 'Municheers', was fulsome. It said in an editorial, 'The instinct of the people today to praise (even to the pitch of extravagance) the peacemakers, is sound'.

Looking back on the files and archives, it is interesting to see that Beaverbrook's *Evening Standard*, almost alone among the Press on that opening day of October 1938, struck a warning note. Its editorial was headed, 'Keep Sane'. It said, 'In the rush of overmastering relief that Britain is saved from war, much can be understood and forgiven. There are dangers, however, in the emotionalism which made London crowds yesterday cheer jubilantly as if every problem had been triumphantly solved for this country by the Munich Pact.'

It is of interest, too, to record that when Britain's pact with

Poland was announced in April 1939, the *Daily Express* was discordant in its disagreement. It was the only paper to question the wisdom of this guarantee. Its editorial of 1 April 1939 said, 'There is no discordant voice anywhere save only from this newspaper. The *Daily Express* regrets 1, that a guarantee should have been given that involved Britain in the concerns of Eastern Europe, 2, that it was given without seeking and obtaining the approval of the Dominions and their concurrence in the obligations. The *Daily Express* opposes the commitment to Poland.'

Three weeks later, on 25 April 1939, we find the *Daily Express* saying, 'This newspaper has stated over and over again its belief that there will be no war now. That remains our conviction. But in stating it recently we have done so with some restraint because we realised the danger of encouraging among the citizens a mood of complacency unfavourable to a stern prosecution of the national effort. Mainly our confidence depends on the vigour and speed with which Britain makes herself strong in arms.'

Of these events, Beaverbrook later said, 'I earnestly desired peace. That was my motive and my aim. Chamberlain asked me to lower the temperature and help keep the peace. I tried to do so. I thought that to prepare for war was the best way of ensuring peace. That is why we struggled to arm the nation. Chamberlain gave me to understand he would not go to war. Even after he gave his pledge to Poland, he had no intention of going to war. He told me so, and his Ministers said the same thing. They believed the Polish pledge would deter Hitler and show him that Britain meant business. If Chamberlain had stuck to his policy as he assured me he would, we should be better off in the world today. When Chamberlain allowed himself to be pushed into war by his colleagues, he should have resigned. He did not believe in the war. He did not wish to join battle. Yet he continued as Prime Minister against his better belief. I am sorry the last war took place. I still maintain it was folly for us to go to war with Germany in 1939.'

It must be remembered that when the *Daily Express* was crying 'no more war' it was also clamouring for more tanks, more planes, more guns, more ships. In strength, the paper said, lies peace.

Many of those who criticized Beaverbrook for his inter-war attitudes would vote no money for arms, would have no conscription, would make no move to rearm the nation until public opinion, at the last moment, was on their side.

Only when opinion, which Beaverbrook had done much to mould, hardened decisively in favour of arms did these critics become such splendid soldiers of the Queen, or rather the King as then it was. At least they all now claim to be called soldiers of the King or Queen.

But it's true to say that not all those stern advocates of war went to war and did the fighting.

11

MACHINES AND MAGIC

Beaverbrook the Patriot

A FRENCHMAN said to me, 'We French cannot forgive the British because after France fell in the last war, you refused to give in. It was bad for our pride. We cannot forget it.'

There is not much gratitude in life. Men and nations often bear a grudge against those who have saved their skins. They hate debts. They take the first chance to repay them by striking hard blows against those to whom they owe salvation.

Beaverbrook put the fighting aircraft which won the Battle of Britain in the sky. Many other people played a part. Churchill, in undying phrases, has paid tribute to the young men who hazarded and often lost their lives clawing from the clouds the invading hosts. Churchill himself, with courage, imagination, and refusal to believe in defeat, played a star part in that drama. Countless unknown men and women at desks, in back rooms, in Government offices, sweated out their strength through long hours of night and dangerous hours of day-time. Many who deserved credit have been denied it amid the debris of history. And in spite of the wasted years between the two wars, men who planned to defy tradition and design Hurricane and Spitfire will ever live in the story of these islands.

Having said all this, it must be recorded that without Beaverbrook the Battle of Britain would have been lost. Time and again, in times of crisis, Britain has thrown up a man to match the hour. Beaverbrook was that man at that hour. And since then carpers and critics, little dogs who yap at the heels of greatness, have taken every chance to belittle his feats and begrudge him his shining hour of history.

Colonel Moore-Brabazon (later Lord Brabazon), who succeeded him as Minister of Aircraft Production, said on 11 July 1941, 'Lord Beaverbrook had to ginger up the aircraft industry, which was particularly complacent, with a tremendous lot of drive. That did not make him popular up and down the industry. When Lord Beaverbrook indulges in operations, he is not very keen on anaesthetics.'

Colonel Brabazon declared that Lord Beaverbrook had robbed every hen-roost up and down the country. He had produced machines which never in any other circumstances could have been made. He ended, 'Lord Beaverbrook is among those to whom the Prime Minister referred when he said that never was so much owed by so many to so few. High upon the scroll of honour of this country must ever remain the name of Max Aitken, first Baron Beaverbrook.' Colonel Moore-Brabazon, who had been Minister of Transport when Lord Beaverbrook was given the job of Minister of Aircraft Production by Churchill in 1940, added, 'I could have murdered him. He swept like Genghis Khan through every department. It was remarkable.'

Beaverbrook said of this period of his life, 'I thought I would be hanged by the Air Marshals if I failed to produce the planes and I thought I would be hanged by the Germans if the country failed. When I started at the Ministry of Aircraft Production, there were too many pilots to fly the planes. After I had been there for a time there were so many planes we couldn't get the pilots to fly them.'

Let figures speak. Beaverbrook, who had been protesting for days that it would be harder to get a Texas mule into a six-foot-by-two stall than to get him into the Government, was appointed on Tuesday, 14 May 1940. It was four days after the Germans had invaded France.

At that time there were only five Spitfires and Hurricanes in reserve behind the front line. If five fighter pilots on that day had had their aircraft damaged in the skies and baled out, there would have been planes on the ground waiting for them to fly. But after that there would have been no more planes. The nation's supply of fighter aircraft would have been exhausted.

In the first four weeks of his duties as Minister, Beaverbrook saw that the pilots at last had enough planes to fly. Before the Battle of Britain was fully joined, the total of aircraft in reserve had risen to 65 per cent of the operational strength of Fighter Command. Also the number of planes with the squadrons had been increased by 50 per cent. By April 1941, in spite of the losses of the Battle of Britain, the reserve in five main operational types of aircraft was 100 per cent.

In the first four months of 1940, 2700 aircraft were built. In the next four months, 6400. This was at a time when the enemy overran France and dominated the Channel from the air. It was at a time when the sea-borne commerce was driven from the southern ports of this country and when, for the first time in the long history of Britain, the Port of London was closed. It was at a time when enemy air strength outnumbered our own by four to one, when German preparations were going on night and day in the French ports for an invasion of this island. The dramatic increase in British air strength of course owed something to preparations made before Beaverbrook took charge of the Ministry of Aircraft Production. Too little credit has been paid to the men who made the preparation. The truth still remains that without the drive and dynamism of Beaverbrook our preparations would have been buried in rubble.

In the year 1939, 500 Hurricanes were built. In the year 1940, 2580.

In 1939, 430 Spitfires took to the skies. In 1940, 1500.

Before Beaverbrook took office there had been no output of repaired aircraft at all. In the next twelve months, 9000 aircraft, most of them fighters, were repaired and once again sent to do their work. Engine production in the British factories was doubled. Furthermore, 12,000 damaged engines were rescued, repaired, and restored to service.

Beaverbrook's Ministry of Aircraft Production was a limb torn from the body of the Air Ministry. Until Beaverbrook's appointment, the Air Marshals had been responsible for supplies of aircraft. The Air Marshals wanted to keep power in their own hands. Beaverbrook had to fight some of them, as well as Goering's hordes.

He took instant, bold decisions. He gave orders for all other construction except that of fighters to be delayed. Fighters only were to be built. He was accused of sabotage, piracy, disruption. He went ahead.

How was it done? When a man is drowning, he lashes out with violence. He tries to drown those who attempt to rescue him. He resists every effort on his behalf. Beaverbrook was confronted with experts who from every corner of the kingdom told him what could not be done. With ruthlessness and force, he smashed every opponent to his plans. He made enemies, but he made aircraft. And in the end he dragged the drowning nation safe to shore. Beaverbrook put the point clearly with his words, 'I am prepared to murder the body of the aircraft industry to prevent it committing suicide by letting the Air Force down'.

Lord Nuffield, with Government money, had built a large factory to produce Spitfires. But the Spitfires were not coming forth at a speed to suit Lord Beaverbrook. Nuffield was also in charge of an organization for the repair of damaged aircraft.

Beaverbrook decided to transfer the control of the Spitfire factory to another firm and to take control of the repairs of damaged aircraft into the hands of his own Ministry.

He said to Alexander Dunbar, the man whom he put in control of the Nuffield factory, 'Costs don't matter. Systems don't matter. Nothing matters but the number of Spitfires you can put into the air in the next six weeks.' Dunbar removed by lorry all the completed components from the Nuffield shadow factory to his own factory 200 miles away in the south. Nuffield's was disrupted. Some believed that long-term production might be affected. But six weeks later, ninety extra Spitfires were in the sky which otherwise could not have been produced so quickly.

Nuffield came to see Beaverbrook and said, 'You have defied me. The last Air Minister who defied me was Lord Swinton. He got the sack. If you defy me, you will get the sack.' Beaverbrook answered, 'There is this difference between myself and Swinton. I like the sack. I want to get it.' He added, 'It will be a relief to be sacked now before I am hanged later for failure to get the aircraft.'

Nuffield then approached Churchill. Nuffield was a big subscriber to the Tory Party. He urged Churchill to intervene. Churchill said, 'I cannot interfere with the manufacture of aircraft'. He turned down Lord Nuffield.

Beaverbrook says of those days, 'Churchill decided to back me. He had given me the job and he trusted me to do it. He said he'd support me right or wrong. And he did. I was sometimes wrong, you know. But Churchill was unswerving.'

At the end of the Nuffield row, Nuffield's representative came to see Beaverbrook at Stornoway House. He tried to push Beaverbrook around, but bounced back with bruises. He stormed off in a rage shouting at Beaverbrook, 'You are the English Quisling'. He repeated this cry around the country.

The production department of the Air Ministry had been dispersed to Harrogate. By the waters of Harrogate some worked hard, others lay down and slept. There came a harsh awakening. Beaverbrook had to choose between moving himself to Harrogate or moving the production department back to London. Beaverbrook did not think the climate of Harrogate would suit him or the war effort. The production department stirred, swore, and shifted. Everyone said it was impossible. Within days it was done.

The attitude of some of the Air Ministry top brass is made plain by this tale. Air Vice-Marshal Freeman, at the time Director of Development at the Ministry of Aircraft Production, was naturally a friend of the men who controlled the Air Ministry. He was about to take off on an inspection tour from a north London airfield. As he mounted the plane, an urgent call reached him to return to the building. He did so. He asked what was the matter? He was told, 'Enemy aircraft are reported. We expect them over the airfield any moment.' Freeman replied, 'Oh, my God, is that all? I thought it was a telephone call from Lord Beaverbrook.'

If telephone calls from Lord Beaverbrook were worse than air raids, he had some cause for his bombing, blitzing technique.

There was the terrible story of Brize-Norton in Oxfordshire. To Brize-Norton new aircraft produced by Beaverbrook and his men were sent for operational purposes. The Air Staff, at the end of June 1940, gave assurances that aircraft were safely dispersed at Brize-Norton. Lord Beaverbrook visited Brize-Norton and violently disagreed with the verdict of the Air Staff. He informed the Prime Minister and the Cabinet that, in his opinion, the aircraft stored there were dangerously exposed to enemy attack, not properly protected from weather conditions, and overcrowded. He pressed for immediate action. The Air Staff, however, took no action.

On 16 August 1940 the evening was cloudy. Out of the clouds came two JU 88s. They dropped bombs at Brize-Norton. They destroyed no less than forty-six aircraft crowded in and around the hangars there.

Next morning a hurricane raged in the Cabinet, and its name was Hurricane Max.

Beaverbrook's will was steeled and his imagination stirred by the death of his son-in-law, Drogo Montagu. He went to the funeral in March 1940. Drogo had flown for ten years before the war. In peacetime he always avoided clouds. In wartime he told his father-in-law how fighting pilots sought clouds for concealment. Drogo found his cloud. He came hurtling out of it and plunged to death on the earth. Nobody knows what happened. He was perhaps shot down by an enemy. Beaverbrook never forgot Drogo Montagu. He was resolute that the young man's friends should not lack tools.

He sent for me during these early days at his Ministry.

Beaverbrook blazed at me. As I saw passion in his eyes, I understood the peril of the nation. Beaverbrook said, 'What you've got to understand is that unless I get fighters in the sky over the next few weeks, there will be no future for this country. We shall get chains or death. Nothing else matters now.'

Churchill gave Beaverbrook a shower of encouragement in private and in public. He exercised a considerable influence over Beaverbrook. Beaverbrook would talk to Churchill as if in the Prime Minister's hands lay the decision how long it would be before the Nazi storm gathering across the Channel began to lash the island. He would say to him, 'Two weeks would be something. Four weeks would mean a lot.'

He telephoned factories, sent personal messages, interviewed men from midnight hour till noonday sun. He had every manager of every factory for air frames and engines report in detail at the end of each day to him personally what shortages were holding up their production.

Handley Page would not work on a Sunday. He was alarmed by Beaverbrook. He was so alarmed that he would not answer the telephone on the Sabbath. Beaverbrook pondered what to do. He did not desire to combat the conscience of a man who was against Sunday work. Then he said, 'Very well. Have Handley Page come and see me at midnight on Sundays. When the Sabbath is over we will start our week's work together.' So Handley Page was made to come and see the Minister on Sunday evenings at 12 o'clock, midnight.

Sunday proved for those without Sabbatarian scruples the best day of work. On this day other Government departments were resting. It left Beaverbrook and his team free to do what they desired without interference from any quarter.

Beaverbrook worked at a tension that would have broken the heart and snapped the nerve of other men. Each night he would telephone to ask Dowding and Air Vice-Marshal Rodney Park, at that time in command of the Number Eleven Group of fighters defending London through August and September, 'How many Spitfires do you need tomorrow? How many Hurricanes?'

All through these days and weeks his son, Max, was in the skies as a fighter pilot. He was one of the best of Britain's bravest. The father would telephone the son in the morning before the day's work and fighting began to wish him God-speed and good luck. In the evening he would await his son's call to tell him all was well. If the call was delayed, the father, while never relaxing his drive ahead, would become restless and anxious.

I remember a conversation with him at this time. He sat, a small figure in a vast armchair, as the summer darkness fell in the skies behind him. He said, 'How many of our young men do you think are swimming in the sea tonight? How many of those pilots are on their rafts in the ocean? It's a terrible time. It's a terrible fate for those young men. Think of the sufferings they endure. Think of the hunger. Think of the lack of sleep and lack of hope. Crucifixion is an easier death than the death those young men have sometimes to die.' The man in the chair, as he spoke, lived through the sufferings of his son, or of some other man's son, should disaster strike them. It was not an act. It was the fuel in that strange engine that drove industry at a pace men believed impossible until it won the race with death.

An issue arose about the armaments on the fighter aircraft. Some said there was a need to replace the .303 machine-guns with 20 mm. cannon. Enemy planes were armouring themselves more and more heavily. Machine-guns could not penetrate the armour. Air Ministry experts flatly declared that machine-guns should continue to be placed in British fighter planes.

An Air Force officer in the Ministry of Aircraft Production stood strongly against the substitution of the cannon for the machine-gun. Beaverbrook talked to a civil servant in that Air Force officer's department. The officer, hearing of this, sent a strong memorandum to the civil servant, forbidding him to discuss such matters with the Minister. Beaverbrook instantly dismissed the Air Force officer.

The Air Ministry protested that it was intolerable for civil servants to have access to the Minister above the heads of officers in command. Beaverbrook stood pat. The Air Force officer went.

Beaverbrook, on his own responsibility, decided to substitute the 20 mm. cannon for the .303 machine-guns as weapons for the aircraft. Air Ministry officials opposed him. Dowding supported him. While the Air Ministry was cursing Beaverbrook for giving up the .303 machine-guns, Dowding was urging him to put in the 20 mm. cannon. They went together to the works where the wings for planes were being made. They said, 'Make 200 wings to hold 20 mm. guns'. That was the start of a revolution in armament for British aircraft. Nobody would go back to machine-guns afterwards. But the courage of this order put the Air Force operational experience with the new weapons forward by many weeks.

Within the first few days of holding office, Beaverbrook stretched his hand across the Channel to France. The death-rattle was in the throat of that nation. Beaverbrook tried to get back the aircraft which had flown there to help defend the country. He failed. Then he heard of the spare parts lying in France designed to mend the planes in action over the French front. Mobilizing transport aircraft in this country, he brought back all these spare parts. He naturally enraged officials who wanted transport planes for their own purposes. But their rage was nothing to his own when he discovered that Captain Peter Macdonald, then Conservative M.P. for the Isle of Wight, had taken one of his planes and brought it back from France with a cargo of officers. He was furious. He said, 'I don't want your damned officers. I want spare parts to build aircraft.'

At the end of two months in office, Beaverbrook was enlisting the industrial might of America. Asked in July 1940 what limit he was putting on orders for aircraft from America, he replied, 'The sky's the limit'. He tried to get Henry Ford to make engines and aircraft. Henry Ford refused, saying he did not wish to make engines for any belligerent. But the Packard Company of Detroit agreed to build Rolls-Royce Merlin engines. The plant and tools were supplied. They built 6000 Merlin engines. This was the first big contract for American machinery to fly the British skies.

Beaverbrook needed aluminium. His plan to get housewives to hand in their aluminium pots and pans to make aircraft was front-page news in all newspapers.

Less public were his affairs with Loew. Mr. Loew was a Jew. He was a designer of machines for fabricating aluminium. He had fled from Hitler's Germany to Bournemouth. There he was making aluminium extrusion presses, machines to extrude aluminium.

He had a crew of seven, all of them Jewish refugees from Germany. When war began, all were interned. But Beaverbrook wanted the machines these seven men could make. He got the ear, nose, and throat specialist, Alexander, another Jew, to go seeking these men. He went from camp to camp from end to end of the country crying. 'Where are those seven missing men?'

Alexander, and a colleague whom he collected in a concentration camp called Charles Blauhorn, mobilized skilled mechanics for aircraft works.

It was like Evangeline, in Longfellow's *Tale of Arcadie*, seeking her lover Gabriel in the Michigan forests. Unlike Evangeline, Alexander and Blauhorn found their men before it was too late.

They were freed. Then M.I.5 protested that they were

dangerous to the nation's welfare. A storm arose. Beaverbrook sought refuge from the storm. He agreed that the whole matter should be decided by a referee. He managed to see that the referee would be his old comrade Lord Bennett (former Prime Minister of Canada). Bennett and Beaverbrook had made up every difference between them. Beaverbrook felt safe. Lord Bennett, after careful weighing of the evidence, decided that M.I.5 was right and Beaverbrook wrong. He wrote a report against Beaverbrook. Beaverbrook ignored the report and kept the men at work with Loew. Bennett was furious. So were many more.

Bennett came to see Beaverbrook and said, 'But I am the referee'. Beaverbrook replied, jokingly, 'I always dispute the decision of the referee'. Bennett took the joke seriously and went towering and stamping out of Beaverbrook's office. He repeated Beaverbrook's words to all who would listen. So that single, ill-considered sentence has stood against Beaverbrook through the years.

Meanwhile, Loew was haunted by fear that the Germans would land in this country and take vengeance on him. His dream was to go to America. He could not get a permit.

By now Beaverbrook was at the Ministry of Supply. He wanted an improvement made in the magazines holding ammunition. He wanted it made possible for the magazines to use .3 (American) ammunition. They were at present only able to use the .303 English size. Supplies of the .3 ammunition were available and magazines had to be adapted to take them.

Beaverbrook said to Loew, 'If you improve these magazines, I will get you a permit for America'. Before long Loew was back with a design to improve the magazines. Beaverbrook said, 'Very well, I will now see you get clearance for America.' Loew refused. He said he had changed his mind and would prefer to stay and share the dangers of the Island with his British friends. He stayed and gave supreme service to Britain.

Beaverbrook's words, his ways, and his work were constantly attacked in Parliament. He could not reply in the House of Commons. He was a peer. But he met his critics of the Commons in a Committee Room of the House. They came in droves. They crammed the doorways and filled the corners. Everyone had his complaint. This was wrong. That was wrong. All was wrong.

Beaverbrook arose after listening to this long tale of grievances and began his speech. 'Everything is all wrong at the Ministry—except Production. And that is all right.'

After the planes had been built, after the blitz had been conquered, after the Battle of Britain had been won, Beaverbrook wanted to retire from Government. Churchill prevailed upon him to stay. But Beaverbrook's health and strength had been shaken by efforts that could have killed a man half his years. In the end he agreed to Churchill's insistence. In May 1941 he became Minister of State, but left the Ministry of Aircraft Production.

During his year of office he had smashed men, smashed methods, smashed old moulds of Civil Service and governmental procedure, but he had saved Britain from a smash.

The thing outstanding was his courage. He ran great risks. He took decisions which, if they had gone wrong, could have lost the war for Britain. He took those decisions always on his own responsibility and often against the strong, vehement, sincere advice of men who had spent a lifetime in the field of aircraft production.

On the day that the big Battle of Britain ended, my telephone rang. The voice of Beaverbrook came to me across the line, 'Peter, do you keep a diary?' In truth Beaverbrook knew that I did not keep a diary. It was a habit he discouraged among those who worked at his side in the inter-war years. He felt that people employed by him who had time to write in diaries could more profitably spend time writing for the *Express* newspapers. Beaverbrook said to me, 'Well, if you had a diary, I would tell you to record in it that this day our country has won a victory that will be recorded in the annals of history in the same terms as Trafalgar or Waterloo are recorded'.

It was this same sense of values which led him to telephone me on the afternoon that Hitler first broke out into the Low Countries and began his invasion to the West. Beaverbrook asked me how the news was coming in and then said, 'You can record in your diary, if you have one, that today Hitler lost the war'.

Everyone else in London at this point seemed to think that Hitler might win the war. His attack and its speed had struck an icicle of foreboding into the warmth of many a brave heart. Beaverbrook went on, 'Hitler's entry into the Low Countries makes the intervention of the United States of America inevitable. I do not know whether he will overrun France. I do not even know if he will attempt to invade this country. But sooner or later now, America will intervene and when America intervenes you can be sure Hitler will be vanquished.'

12

MAX AND THE MONARCHY

Beaverbrook the Subject

BEFORE the last line and final shade of this portrait of my friend, Max Beaverbrook, is given, it is right to attempt to show something of his attitude to Kings, as well as to the King of Kings.

Some have suggested that Beaverbrook had a vendetta against different members of the British Monarchy. What truth is there in this charge?

During the crisis over the abdication of Edward VIII, Beaverbrook fought strongly on the side of the Monarch. He was on a liner half-way across the Atlantic when he received word that the King wished him to return. He returned on the same liner and stood at the King's side through the travail and torment of those days.

The truth must now be told that Baldwin, who was Prime Minister at the time when the new King succeeded his father, was informed, when King George V died, by two of the new King's intimate advisers, that he was going to marry Mrs. Simpson. Baldwin said nothing for six months. But he intended to dethrone the King. He said to Churchill, long days before the crisis broke upon the land, 'The Yorks will do the job very well'.

'Possibly', Beaverbrook said later, 'Baldwin was convinced he was right to get rid of King Edward VIII. He may have perceived instabilities in the Monarch which, as Prime Minister, he felt had to be taken into account. But it is certain that he intended to turn him out long before relations with Mrs. Simpson came to a crisis.

'Now the King need not have abdicated. He could have gone to Windsor Castle. He could have pulled up the drawbridge and kept the world at bay. He could have married the lady and cocked a royal snook at Baldwin, the Archbishop of Canterbury and at the masses arrayed against him.'

Indeed this is the course of action that when the King spoke with his friends like Beaverbrook he had undertaken to follow. He told Beaverbrook in clear terms this was his intention.

One Friday evening, Beaverbrook told me, the King invited Churchill to dine with him. At dinner he gave Churchill no indication of his intention to abdicate. After dinner Churchill came to see Beaverbrook. It was 2 o'clock in the morning. Churchill and Beaverbrook conferred together and Churchill gave Beaverbrook certain advice.

The wintry sun arose and later that morning a Cabinet Minister came to see Beaverbrook. He said, 'The King has abdicated'. Beaverbrook went round to Churchill and told him the news. Churchill refused to believe it. He said, 'Nonsense'. He repeated that the King had given him no such indication on the previous evening, the very last night of his Kingship. Then Churchill made a statement to the Press urging patience from the people. It was an unfortunate statement because the King had already abdicated, though Churchill refused to believe it. And Beaverbrook could not reveal to Churchill that a Cabinet Minister had given him the news because he had promised not to disclose this source of information to anybody.

Beaverbrook was provoked by the uncertainties created by the vacillations of the Monarch. Churchill had a more spacious spirit. It is not known by everybody that it was Churchill who helped the King to prepare his abdication speech. 'The woman I love' is marked with Churchill's touch.

When the speech was delivered over the radio, elements had drifted in after Churchill had seen it. The King paid compliments to Baldwin. It was a modern version 'Caesar, I about to die salute you'. Except that this time the King was the gladiator condemned to death and Baldwin was the boss who had turned down his thumb.

Meanwhile, Beaverbrook came in for a considerable measure of abuse from those who objected to his supporting the King. But when the Duke of York succeeded his brother and when the day of Coronation came, I saw Lord Beaverbrook pulling on his patent leather side-boots and donning his court dress with the utmost good humour. He set off to the Abbey, declaring, 'I'm going to go to the Coronation and I'm going to enjoy every minute of it'. He did. And from that day until his death his public praise and support of the lady who was first Duchess of York and then Queen of this country and now the Queen Mother has been steadfast and bountiful. Also of her daughter, the Queen.

King George V's own attitude to his children may have had some bearing on the tragedy of the Abdication and the wrenches and strains to nation and family that followed. King George V was an upright man. His ideas of duty and loyalty were firm and fixed.

One of his closest friends was the late, great, Lord Derby. Lord Derby arranged that his son should go to Oxford with the then Prince of Wales (now Duke of Windsor) so the two young men might become friends. Indeed it was Lord Derby who picked Magdalen College as the most suitable college to receive them.

Sir Harold Nicolson told Randolph Churchill,[1] 'Derby was distressed by the way King George bullied his children, and he ventured one day at Knowsley, where they were walking up and down the terrace, to raise the subject, justifying his remarks on the ground that he was the King's oldest friend. He said what delightful companions his own children had become for

[1]*Lord Derby, 'King of Lancashire'*, p. 159.

him when they grew up, and begged the King to realize that they were on the verge of manhood and that he was missing very much in life by frightening them and continuing to treat them as if they were naughty schoolboys. Lord Derby told me the King remained silent for some four minutes after this, and then said, "My father was frightened of his mother. I was frightened of my father, and I'm damned well going to see to it that my children are frightened of me." '

The charge has often been made that Beaverbrook's newspapers suppressed news of Lord Mountbatten. Reference to the files of the *Daily Express* in Fleet Street showed that in truth 1700 references to Lord Mountbatten appeared in the *Express* newspapers from the end of the last war until 1963, an average of one reference every four days for eighteen years.

Beaverbrook himself expressed his attitude to Lord Mountbatten in a newspaper article on 6 May 1962. He wrote, 'As long as Lord Mountbatten was not engaged in political activities no reference [in the *Express*] was unfavourable and the great number were in outspoken praise of him.

'When Lord Mountbatten became a politician he dealt with issues which aroused violent controversy, and particularly those projects furthering the liquidation of the British Empire. He naturally became the object of attack and denunciation.

'But after he was appointed Chief of the Staff, and when it became apparent that he was not engaging in party politics, the *Express* did not attack him.

'What else but opposition to Lord Mountbatten could have been expected when he was delegated by Lord Attlee and the Socialist Government to preside over the partition of India and the liquidation of Indian association with the Empire or Commonwealth?

'And here let me say, nor could I have been expected to agree with Lord Mountbatten's policy in relation to Burma and Malaya. Not even with his decision to deny assistance to the Dutch plan to recapture Indonesia. But that era is past and gone, and there is no use in raising controversy about events long since relegated to the pages of history.'

Sitting in a chair at his home in Surrey, Beaverbrook, in the summer of 1962, amplified his point: 'I looked after the interests of Mountbatten for a long time. I provided him with some of his staff during the war. I sent him Frank Owen, a brilliant newspaperman. But as soon as the war was over, he began to hand out the colonies to people I regarded as the wrong people. The Dutch left Indonesia. That seemed to me to be what he wanted. It was the same with other countries. He embraced those who had been our enemies, the men who had been involved with the Japanese, and set them up in high places. He's an anti-colonialist. Then he went to India. Giving away India wasn't my idea. I wanted to help the Indians to find many years of good government as a united country. I wanted to see that sub-continent, half Moslem, half Hindu, run the right way as a unit and not divided. I attacked Mountbatten over India. At the end of that time I ceased to attack him and frequently praised him. That is the truth about my attitude to Mountbatten.' Some might believe that whatever views we held about the British Empire, none dare deny the quality of action that led to its liquidation. In the whole long history of humanity, the British Empire is the only one that has been given away by its own people after its enemies have been smashed and broken.

Critics of Beaverbrook said he was an enemy of the Duke of Edinburgh. Beaverbrook replied, 'I am perfectly friendly to him. It is on the record that years ago when he applied for British nationality and wanted to keep it secret, I conspired with others to keep that secret.' Beaverbrook felt that the Duke of Edinburgh had more than once expressed his opinion on political matters. This he was entitled to do. But, said Beaverbrook, in the position which he holds in the country, his views carry special weight in certain quarters. And if a man steps into the political arena he must expect to find political opposition from those who disagree with him. The Duke of Edinburgh was first rebuked on 15 November 1953 for this kind of politicking. He had publicly advocated conscription. *Reynolds News* of that day said as follows, 'This newspaper hopes that the Duke will not be misled by false friends into thinking he can speak out freely on controversial topics, or can express general approval of one side or the other. The strength of the Throne lies in its political neutrality. We all want to keep it that way.'

In November 1960 the Duke of Edinburgh spoke at an Anglo-German dinner. He made a plea for concord between Germany and Britain. He urged that Britain must play her full part in the European Community.

Many will agree with these views of the Duke. Many will disagree. But all will know that he spoke in clear terms on a political issue that arouses deep feelings in a multitude of hearts.

Of this speech to the Anglo-German Society and the interest and attitude it represents, Beaverbrook said, 'I have no more concern in the Duke of Edinburgh except for his apparent concern in the Common Market. If he lays off the Common Market, I'll lay off him. If he goes back to the Common Market, I'll lay on to him again. It's a matter of political belief and action. Apart from this, I am in no sense his enemy.' He added, 'And the paper that opposes his political utterances is by no means a "bloody awful newspaper" on that account.'

In modern times Beaverbrook's attitude to Royalty seemed to be that they should keep out of politics, but that if they went into them they must expect the rough-and-tumble treatment, neither more nor less, which comes to others.

The Duke of Edinburgh, in politics, seemed to hold views far apart from the Peer, Lord Beaverbrook.

On 23 March 1962 *Time* magazine reported as follows: 'After proving himself a consummate goodwill ambassador during the first month of a seven-week trade-drumming tour of South America, Britain's Prince Philip stumbled with a veritable gaffe-and-a-half at Paraguay's Government House. "It's a pleasant change", off-handed His Royal Highness to President Alfredo Stroessner, "to be in a country which isn't ruled by its people." As the continent's sole surviving dictator glowered around the room and underlings intently began to contemplate their fingernails, Philip quickly thought to recoup by implying that he was merely expressing his pleasure at temporarily escaping Britain's "Lord's Day Observance Society", which perennially criticizes the Royal Family for attending sports events on a Sunday. "Here", beamed the peripatetic Prince, "the Government decides what is to be done—and it is done." '

Beaverbrook added about the Duke of Edinburgh, 'His political pronouncements disturb me. It is my firm belief that the Common Market, which he supports, will in effect destroy the remnants of the system of Imperial Preference, and on that account the structure of the British Empire or Commonwealth if you prefer it.'

Almost all the criticisms of the Duke of Edinburgh which have appeared in the *Express* have been written by John Gordon of the *Sunday Express*. He is a writer of force and independence. His views are his own. If he were not given freedom, he would not write any more in the *Express* newspapers. In a candid moment Beaverbrook said, 'I never read John Gordon until Sunday morning'. He added with a laugh, 'And I don't *always* read him then. But I always enjoy him when I do.'

I hold no brief for Duke or Peer. Neither needs my brief, and neither would heed my views on politics. But it is important for men to understand Beaverbrook's attitude to the consort of our Queen.

Beaverbrook got the worst of two worlds. He was charged with denying his writers' liberty. When he gave them liberty, he was liable to be blamed for what they wrote.

13

BEHAVIOUR AND BELIEF

Beaverbrook the Christian

BEAVERBROOK once said the late Lloyd George was a man 'almost free from the blemish of human weakness'. Lloyd George said that Beaverbrook was 'a very religious man'.

On this evidence, Lloyd George was a better judge of character than Beaverbrook.

If you dined at Cherkley, you could see, silhouetted on the skyline facing your host's chair, a cross. He did not talk much about it. But he looked at it. It was always there before him. That wooden cross was a deeper part of him than the big brass band he conducted daily across the nation with his Press.

People doubt this. A lady said to me not long ago, 'How dare he have a cross on his land? How dare he write a book about Christ? His face is so ugly. A person with that face *can't* be a Christian.' If that is to be the yardstick of judgement, many of us must dread the day of Reckoning—including this lady. But this is typical of the bigotry that has assassinated so many characters in our generation.

Enemies say that Beaverbrook's quotations from the Scriptures, his pursuit of moral standards in public which he certainly did not always live in private, his hatred of persecution and bigotry, were sham. They say he used religion as a cloak of respectability to conceal the carcass of corruption beneath.

This is false. The deepest and most constant note in Beaverbrook's life was always his belief in Christ. Those who knew the surface of the man, without studying the secret depths, may find this statement unbelievable or exaggerated. It remains a fact, confirmed by years of experience working at his side in days grey and gay, sad and glad, when pressures of every kind were upon him. He was like a fish on a hook. He leaped, struggled, often ran away. But the barb was in him.

When I worked on his newspapers, I had no faith myself. One night it fell to my lot to remain on duty in the office when all others left. A senior executive, as he said good-night, told me, 'Peter, I'm tired. Don't telephone me unless big news breaks.' In the foolish fashion of youth I replied, 'What story will be big enough for me to waken you? Christ coming back to earth?' The executive stopped in his tracks. He turned to me and said, 'Peter, He comes back for me every day of my life'.

Finding it droll that this man should take a view which at the time I felt childish, I told Beaverbrook what had happened. I thought he would be amused. He was not. He was angry. He was angry at me for daring to think that such a statement of faith was anything but the most important statement that had been made that day, or for many days, in Fleet Street. His low growl of comment showed his distaste of my mockery.

In the mid-thirties, I heard Beaverbrook talking with Geoffrey Gilbey, who at that time wrote about racing in his newspapers. Beaverbrook was helping Gilbey write an article praising the work of the Oxford Group which was then coming into the forefront of the news. This was the first time I had heard anything about the Oxford Group. I was hit by the force and power of Beaverbrook's advocacy. Gilbey, when this ended, said to Beaverbrook, 'You feel so strongly about this sort of thing that I think you ought to join in with them and help them'. Beaverbrook replied, 'Geoffrey, I am a Scottish Presbyterian. The faith of my fathers is good enough for me.' Then he turned and gave me a big wink.

When the Oxford Group was granted its name by the Board of Trade, Oliver Stanley, then President of the Board of Trade, telephoned Beaverbrook, asking his advice. Beaverbrook thrust his head fiercely towards the telephone. It looked as if he wished to wriggle down it and reach Stanley over the wires. He barked, 'For Heaven's sake, Oliver, keep your head out of that nest of hornets. Leave it alone. Let them have their name. They're entitled to it.'

He had a high and healthy regard for people who fought all out for their convictions. His conception of 'Jesus, meek and mild' was that it is a misconception. This he made plain in his book, *The Divine Propagandist*. Anyone who wishes to understand the root and heart of Beaverbrook, should study *The Divine Propagandist*. When a friend asked him, 'How long did you take to write this book?' Beaverbrook replied, 'Thirty years'. The length of the book is seventeen thousand words. It meant an output of about one and a half words a day. Beaverbrook meant that thirty years of life's convictions were recorded in that volume.

His answer to this person was like Whistler's answer to the judge. Whistler, the artist, suing a critic for libel, told the judge that he charged five hundred guineas for a picture which took just over two hours to paint. The judge said, 'Do you mean to say you charge five hundred guineas for two hours' work?' Whistler replied, 'No, my Lord. For a lifetime of experience.'

Beaverbrook's Christ is a fighting Christ. His Christ is not a personality Who stands aside from the world and condemns those who stumble. It is a personality Who for three intensive, vigorous, relentless years stamped His truth upon all ages. Beaverbrook says of Him, 'It is one thing to be kindly and gentle and pitiful. It is quite another thing to compromise and betray vital interests of the soul or the State for the sake of being gentle. . . . Jesus as a propagandist might be described as well-nigh merciless.' He adds, 'All propaganda which is powerful and effective must be combative in character. It must increase in intensity and it proceeds until ultimately it reaches a tone not far removed from violence.'

Beaverbrook's Christ, as portrayed in *The Divine Propa-*

gandist, is an original Christ. It is a picture by 'a man of affairs—one of the worldly men of my generation'.

It is a picture painted with reverence. It is a picture that is deeply moving to any perceptive heart. Beaverbrook speaks of Tim Healy, his old Catholic friend, who told him, 'Our old monks kept a separate pen to write the name of God and did so always on their knees'.

It is a picture that is sincere. He speaks of 'trying to understand Jesus in the flickering light of a limited intelligence and certainly restricted research'. But he adds, 'It is the right of the man who has lived in the market place to outline the sermons of Christ as he conceives them, if he feels the disposition to declare himself and his faith'.

Few modern men have guts today to do it. Those who stand up in positions of power and wealth to declare a faith are open to sneer and jibe. They are accused of insurance against hell-fire. They are accused of hypocrisy. What they believe is compared by critics with how they are said to have behaved.

Beaverbrook, by publishing *The Divine Propagandist*, risked an egging from his enemies. He was a man who again and again had hurled eggs at his own foes. Tomatoes were also thrown in their direction, often with accuracy, always with cunning, sometimes unfairly, sometimes with a chunk of granite inside them, sometimes more painful because they have been inside a tin. But Beaverbrook was not guilty of the acid calm and glacial venom of the character assassins abroad in this century who, like Judas, are out to destroy the best. There was always a grin behind the grenade, a hand outstretched not far behind the tornado of tomatoes and explosion of eggs.

The publication of *The Divine Propagandist* was the best and bravest act of Beaverbrook's life.

He interprets the Kingdom of Heaven as happiness, a happiness within a heart which does not depend on money or place. He says, 'If you prefer personal safety to your faith, you will lose the Kingdom of real happiness'. He rejects St. John's 'fanaticism'. He rejects St. Paul's 'intellectualism'. He believes St. Paul used his brain to complicate and confuse the simplicity of Christ's message. He says that Jesus 'set His face against what may be called public asceticism and Puritanism'.

It is on record that Christ went without drink in a hot desert for forty days. Without food also. It is hard not to regard this as public asceticism.

But 'asceticism' and 'Puritanism' are not popular in an age where perversion and adultery have become acceptable, and where the most forceful propagandists of society insist on a man drinking what they decide and smoking what they choose, or risking social sneers if he refrains.

Beaverbrook says, with truth, that a glum, unhappy, sour-spirited Christian is not living his faith to the full. It is St. Paul's 'taboos' that offend him. He says of the Saint, 'Jesus has sympathy and forgiveness instead of the Pauline anathema . . . [St. Paul] has no use for the all-embracing Fatherhood of God which makes all men the same to Jesus'.

It is difficult for an ordinary man to explain how those who knew Jesus well on earth accepted so soon and so readily St. Paul's leadership, had his outlook been as far from that of his Master as Beaverbrook believed. St. Paul took sin seriously. He faced the damaging effect of evil on men and nations. He did not believe a man's private life was only his private affair.

If you go to a tailor, you expect him to cut his cloth to suit your own shape and size. But if you want to wear Christ's garment, you have to cut your size and shape to fit it. It means yielding wrong and embracing right. A small sense of sin means a small sense of Christ.

All this is uncomfortable. It may interfere with your pleasure. This seems to be one reason why the British Lord was doubtful about the Jewish Saint.

On money, Beaverbrook declares that Christ was no Communist. He did not demand that everybody should hand over wealth and property to a common pool. He urged one rich man whose gold was his god to get rid of it. He said that anything—money, sex, career—which governed a man instead of God, must go. Those who had or made money were expected to use it in trust for unselfish purposes, not to spend their life in pursuit of it.

Beaverbrook defines Christ's temptations in the wilderness as 'the purely sensual appeal . . . to turn stones into bread . . . the suggestion that Jesus should perform a sensational and quite useless miracle—which has been called the appeal to spiritual vainglory . . . an offer . . . of all the kingdoms of the Earth in return for an act of formal submission to a power not of God'. He describes the Devil as saying, 'All you have to do is to turn your back on the plain dictates of God and submit yourself to a Counsellor who has a better or more reasonable plan'.

A Liverpool docker, a working man, a simple man, and not the intellectual whom Lord Beaverbrook eyed warily, put this truth in clear terms. He said, 'There are two voices in my heart—a good 'un and a bad 'un. I need to take time each day to throw out the bad 'un and let in the good.'

Beaverbrook boils at the commercialization of Christ by some of the Churches. Indeed, he is watchful of the danger of all 'organized' religion. He says, 'A religion organized into a community, a creed, and a vested interest is in permanent danger of becoming an absolute impediment to the entry into the Kingdom of God'.

Beaverbrook refers briefly to the compassion and forgiveness of the story of the woman taken in adultery. But like so many commentators, he leaves out the last instruction of Jesus to the woman, 'Sin no more'. He is prone to reject what makes him uncomfortable and to find in Jesus what he most desires and believes will make him happy.

'My ways are not your ways, neither are My thoughts your thoughts', said the Lord. The acceptance of Christ's challenge means the yielding of many human values.

Christ said, 'I came not to do My will, but the will of Him

who sent Me'. For the last two thousand years, Christians have been trying to forget this uncomfortable sentiment. They attempt to control Christ to their own comfort. They choose their own pattern of days and ways and call for Christ's blessing on that pattern. It is, 'My will be done, My Kingdom come'. Many balk at the Cross. Many try to control it. Many in early years bet their lives against the truth of it—but as shadows lengthen, try to hedge their bet.

Beaverbrook was not like this. *The Divine Propagandist* reveals a sensitivity, a tenderness, a depth in Lord Beaverbrook which, allied to his understanding of humanity, could have been his greatest asset. It was hard for so masterful a man to accept a Master. It could have been the crown of his days.

Beaverbrook puts most formal church-goers to shame by his written declaration of faith. Few, if any, of his critics have had courage or understanding to print so boldly, humbly, compellingly the deepest convictions of their heart. But when all this is said, there is an element missing in Beaverbrook's Christ.

He is a loving Christ, a forgiving Christ, a joyful Christ, a human Christ (in the sense that he has a deep understanding and love of humanity), an interesting Christ, a passionate Christ, a winning Christ. It is the picture of a man of power, a Gandhi-like figure, who gave truth, defied authority, chose death before worldly triumph. But he is a Christ who never would have been crucified. He is a Christ who did not challenge the compromise and sin of the world. He is a Christ who would have ended up as President of an industrial combine, General Secretary of the Seamen's Union of the Lake of Galilee, or possibly the proprietor of a great chain of newspapers.

Percy Cudlipp, one of Beaverbrook's Editors, once had considerable difficulty in reaching his master on the telephone. He was always told by the man who answered the telephone that Beaverbrook was out riding. One night at dinner this Editor asked George Malcolm Thomson, a close colleague of Lord Beaverbrook for many years, what exactly went on when

Beaverbrook mounted his horse and set forth. Thomson said, 'Well, we give the horses apples or carrots. Then Lord Beaverbrook mounts his horse and I mount mine. Lord Beaverbrook rides ahead. I follow behind. Lord Beaverbrook is like Napoleon. I am like Marshal Ney.' The Editor replied, 'You mean Marshal Yea, George. Marshal Yea.'

It was a good joke. One of the best Percy Cudlipp ever made. It is not marred by the fact that it is unfair to George Malcolm Thomson. He is a man who holds views of his own in thunder and in sunshine. In the face of Lord Beaverbrook's stern, strong disapproval, his sadness and dismay, he dared to vote against Churchill and for the Socialists in 1945. He has been heard to declare that he has lived to regret it. Lord Beaverbrook, with barb and jeer, always tried to keep that regret lively in his colleague. For in truth Beaverbrook preferred men to say 'yea'. And his Christ was a Person who said 'yea' not 'nay' to him.

All of us fall short of glory. When the final edition is published, when the real news appears on the front page for the universe to see, when all those who have criticized others for 'sharing their sins in public', but who have earned a fat living for years by sharing other people's sins in public, find their own shortcomings illumined in the everlasting light, my belief is Lord Beaverbrook may prove a more wholesome story than the story of some of his critics. Certainly it will be more interesting reading. Beaverbrook quotes biblical authority for those who are honest about their faults. It comes in St. James 5, verse 16: 'Confess your faults one to another, and pray one for another, that ye may be healed.' He believes in the guidance of God. He says, 'The Ascension leaves us with the Holy Ghost as our guide. This means that the Divine Spirit can still inspire all our thoughts and actions.' The question remains for us all, 'How much, how definitely and how often do we obey Him?' Obedience is the secret of lasting happiness.

He was a man of deep feeling. Once, walking on the hillside, he pointed to the house of a friend and said, 'They've not been to see me for six months'. I said I was sorry. Beaverbrook replied, 'Sorry? Sorry? They only come to see me when they want money. It's a damn good thing they don't come to see me.' The pain in his voice told of hurts that this man of power had suffered and endured through years of tempest and triumph.

His father, Minister of the Scottish Presbyterian Church, for years preached the gospel in Canada. After his son, Max, had made money, he went to his father and said, 'You can resign now. You are getting old. Making sermons has become a burden. I can look after you and would like to do so.' The father looked at his son and answered, 'Gladly'. Then he said, 'I've been preaching the gospel a long time now. The trouble is that at the end of it all I find myself gazing into the gathering mist.'

The son at that moment saw that his father did not know where he stood. Some of the old pillars had fallen. Old dogmas had crumpled into dust in his mind. He was troubled and confused as he faced the last miles of life's journey.

Beaverbrook's declaration of faith in the evening of his life is a different story. But that conversation with his father had an influence that lasted for nearly sixty years.

14

STEEL AND STRAW

Beaverbrook the Total

NOT long before Lord Beaverbrook's death, my wife and I were his guests.

The arrow was far sped. Its flight dipped towards the final mark. Lord Beaverbrook was almost eighty-five. In the normal span of expectancy not long was left. It is true that he appeared to think he would live for ever. He worked. He enjoyed the sunshine days and sparkling nights. He gloried in gay company. He told a reporter of *Time* magazine, 'I am an old man and should be ready to go—but I am not'.

This final decision was in the hands of the Master of the world, not those of the master of machines, money, and magic of Fleet Street. But when that masterful man at last stood face to face with his own Master, the sharp sword he wielded so boldly, the glittering array of trophies that dangled at his belt, the gold, the power, the ermine, the load of human glory would be of no avail. Even his fearlessness could not help. For the fear of the Lord is the beginning of wisdom.

'The Jones Boys' and 'My Grandfather's Clock' were among Lord Beaverbrook's best songs. He loved the 23rd psalm. He also delivered in ringing tones a predestination hymn of the Church:

> Father, I know that all my life
> Is portioned out for me.
> The changes that are sure to come
> I do not ask to see.

But the change that I and a host of witnesses that encompassed him asked to see was for the Baron to crown the massive achievements of his lifetime by yielding in the battle for his everlasting soul, by putting the Cross of Christ before all else, including the circulation figures of his newspaper.

His old enemy Baldwin used to predict, 'Before he is through, he'll become an evangelist—and a madman'. He was far from lunacy, but could have harried the ghost of Baldwin by making the first part of that prophecy come true.

In the evening, sitting in his chair as long shadows fell across the garden, he said, 'Was I too bitter with Baldwin? Did I hit him too much below the belt? I did make the road hard for him, you know. I think he deserved more than he got. But after all, he was Prime Minister of the country.' Then with a laugh he cried, 'A glorious fellow, Baldwin. Glorious. Glorious. If you talk of hatred, he had it. He loved his hatred of me.'

What was the good and what was the bad in the Baron? There are plenty of rumours and many a report to indicate wicked deeds and dark ways. But when you try to track them down, often, if not usually, it ends in smoke, wind, and dust. It blows up. Nothing is there.

He had a strong love of humanity. He was constant in his demand for humanity from his newspapers. Perhaps it sprang from memory of those early struggling years—the uncertainty and fear of hardship, the wonder and bedazzlement of success. He described in words moving to the human heart the amazement at his first banquet, when he saw the glory of flowers, the glow and gleam of silver, the starshine of diamonds in women's hair.

He would tell how he and his young wife, Gladys, were bewildered at the wonder of their first sight of Paris (the wife wearing the engagement ring that cost her man five dollars before he put the great issue of finance to the test and won the struggle for wealth). How Kipling took them both to Cherkley, and they lay on the lawn contemplating that vast pile, with

Gladys nervous at the size of it all. They bought the place. They were persuaded that no heat was needed in it and in winter it was cold as a Highland loch. There was one telephone hanging on a sort of string. A clanging bell summoned young Aitken from far places in garden or house at the run as calls came from his business associates in Canada across the ocean.

It was here that he brought up his children, acting as both mother and father to them after the death of Gladys in 1927. To the last, walking in the sunshine, he cursed and blenched if he saw some foolish woman neglecting the safety or welfare of some young child.

He did not always have his way. There were setbacks, and serious setbacks, in his life. The first was an experience which made a mark that lasted. At the age of seventeen, he was a law student at Saint John, New Brunswick. He formed a friendship with a young man called Heber Vroom. This young man was a figure of importance in Saint John society. He asked Max Aitken whether he would like to receive an invitation to the annual Assembly Hall—the social event of the year in those days.

The suggestion was received with glory. Young Max was in ecstasy. He hired himself a dress-suit from a tailor. There was white tie, starched collar, and all the trappings for the fray.

But no invitation came. Max waited. And waited. At last he could bear it no more. Almost at the hour when the ball began, he spoke to Heber Vroom and said, 'I've had no invitation'. 'I'm sorry to have to tell you', said Vroom, 'that you were a newsboy at Newcastle and they do not feel they can have a newsboy at the ball.'

Aitken dressed himself up, looked lovingly in the mirror at the hired peacock's plumes, then doffed them and returned them to the tailor. 'It's true I had been a newsboy,' said Beaverbrook, 'but it was hard on a boy of seventeen.'

Another setback came in 1915. He wanted to get a job in Asquith's first Coalition Government. Bonar Law told him this would not be well received as he was young and with no Parliamentary performance behind him. It was true. But truth sometimes adds pepper not balm to the sting of disappointment.

In 1916 there was the setback when Lloyd George offered him the Board of Trade, and then withdrew the offer. Those hours of waiting with no word from the Prime Minister brought into that tough but hungry heart memories of hours of waiting in far-off Saint Joan when a seventeen-year-old student had no word from his friend Heber Vroom.

In 1922, when Bonar Law became Prime Minister, Beaverbrook hoped for a job. But he was so hated by the Big Moguls of the Tory Party who had remained loyal to Lloyd George, that it would have embarrassed Law to give his friend a place. Beaverbrook felt the force of this. So he stood down.

Again this was a crushing blow. Success in newspapers did not quite make up for it. Beaverbrook wanted the power of office.

From 1929 to 1931 Empire Free Trade seemed almost within grasp. But Baldwin dished Beaverbrook each time one way or another. Then from 1931 to 1932, with the financial crisis and the formation of the National Government, all question of tariffs disappeared. R. B. Bennett's statements after he became Prime Minister of Canada fearfully damaged the cause of Empire Free Trade.

By 1940 Beaverbrook did not want office. Churchill has recorded how he had to wheedle and heave Beaverbrook into the Government. It was even an embarrassment to Beaverbrook to undertake the task. But he did and Britain reaped the gain.

In 1945 electoral defeat for Churchill was another setback, and disappointment for Beaverbrook. But it was not so personal a matter and did not cut so deep.

In the course of this up-and-down, bounce-and-bruise journey in life, Beaverbrook mastered the art of personal diplomacy. His powers of persuasion were dangerous and bewitching. Wrath and tenderness, bribe and blackmail, all played their part. He wore resistance away like the dripping of a Chinese torture. He had a genius for his own way and when he met resistance was outwardly unhappy and asthmatic if he could not conquer it, inwardly scornful if he did.

People said he was tough, harsh, and brimful of malice. One way to judge a man is to look at his immediate circle. As they regard him, so he often is. Beaverbrook, with the exception of Churchill, was the sole survivor of those who sat in the Cabinets of Britain in both World Wars. Churchill was his friend. Lloyd George in a lesser degree was so. Bonar Law, Arnold Bennett, H. G. Wells, Rudyard Kipling were close to him. With the exception of Kipling the friendships lasted through lifetime.

The only one Beaverbrook lost was Kipling. When Beaverbrook took up the cause of Ireland and became an advocate of Home Rule for the South, Kipling broke with him. He regarded it as betrayal. He refused to have any more to do with him.

Once at a dinner-party for Smuts in Sir Abe Bailey's home, Beaverbrook, who was with Churchill, met Kipling. Kipling spoke coldly to both men. Beaverbrook, trying to make peace, said, 'Which of us do you dislike most, Churchill or me?' Without hesitation Kipling replied, 'Churchill. And my feeling for you is like an afterglow in the sky when the sun is set.'

Beaverbrook tried again and again for reconciliation, but never found it. It was Kipling who gave his cousin Baldwin the phrase about the Harlot, which Baldwin used against Beaverbrook at the famous meeting at Caxton Hall.

Beaverbrook was invited to the funeral of Kipling, and went. He said, 'I went there with a heavy heart. It was tough to lose him. He was a hard man. He admired strength more than virtue. He said very harsh things. But he said them all with such life and spirit that it was good anyway.'

Stornoway House between the wars was the scene of the liveliest society in London. There were entertained beauties of the day, brains of the century, writers, artists, political leaders of every party.

A light shone over the door at night. It was like the light above Big Ben. When Big Ben's light is shining, it means that Parliament is in session. When the Stornoway House light shone it meant that the party was in session and it cried 'Come in' to all those who were intimates.

There was endless political discussion and it is true that Beaverbrook was brewing much mischief.

Churchill came often. Brendan Bracken was almost always there, with flaming hair, glasses like the headlamps of a motor-car and the torrential, scintillating flow of his talk.

Aneurin Bevan, named by Castlerosse the 'Bollinger Bolshevik', would loll against the mantelpiece, champagne in his hand, again and again informing the host who had given it to him, 'Max, you are so dangerous. I will hang you if I become Prime Minister.'

Some newspapermen employed by him would be welcome to Stornoway at these night sessions. Things heard and seen there were not printed. Beaverbrook, who gathered news as a pigeon pecks clover into its crop, taught all his men to keep confidences.

Former *Daily Express* men are sprinkled all over Fleet Street. When Lord Southwood ('Old Blackout' is one affectionate title bestowed on him by Beaverbrook; another is 'Lord Snow-white') started his reorganization of the *Daily Herald*, he took five members of the *Express*, top men, to help him do it. They went from choice not necessity.

But many work a lifetime on the *Express*. They stay there because they like it. They are loyal and devoted. And they are pensioned nobly when they go. Christiansen, a great editor, was given a gift of £30,000 and an annual income of £3000 when he departed from the *Express*. The pensions list of the *Express* newspapers is large.

The image of Beaverbrook in the mind of many is that of an arch-apostle of materialism. Yet he gave away vast sums. The *Daily Express* was his main work for many years. And he took no money from it. He did not own one share in the *Express* newspapers. He parted from them all many years ago.

A trust known as the Beaverbrook Foundations owns 52 per cent of the voting shares in the *Express*. The directors of these Foundations are Sir Max Aitken (Beaverbrook's son), Lady Beaverbrook, John Gordon, William Barkley, Mrs. Stickney (Beaverbrook's sister), Tom Blackburn (Chairman of Beaverbrook Newspapers), and A. G. Millar (also a Director of Beaverbrook Newspapers).

These Foundations distribute the income in various ways. All retired or ageing Presbyterian Ministers in England receive gifts from them.

Large educational gifts are also given—books to libraries, paintings to galleries.

The Beaverbrook Foundations also own a share in the operating company of Beaverbrook's farms in Somerset. Max Aitken also owns part. The farms are profitable. They are run by a New Zealander called Copland who has the remaining interest in the operating company.

It will be seen therefore that the fruit of Beaverbrook's labours was handed over to others in Britain. And this is the reply to those who have been heard to say that Beaverbrook gave too much to his birthplace, New Brunswick, and too little to Britain, the land which provided him with his platform, his peerage, and his eminence in politics. The story goes that Beaverbrook liked to be a big toad in a small New Brunswick puddle. That he 'discovered' New Brunswick late in life.

In fact, he began his educational charities in New Brunswick in 1909, before he came to Britain. And they continued ever afterwards on a rapidly expanding scale. He gave four skating rinks, bells for churches, libraries, town halls. His gifts to the place of his birth, including scholarships and buildings, were more than twenty million dollars. There is also in Canada another Foundation, the Beaverbrook Canadian Foundation, which pays pensions to all retired Presbyterian Ministers in the Maritime Provinces as well as providing many scholarships and educational grants there. He founded his factories in Canada. When he left there to come to England he was already a very wealthy man. He founded basic industries in Canada—power, steel, cement, and grain elevators. Every one of them is flourishing.

He always with pride kept his roots in his native land. He was a Canadian who was resident in England. He joined the Canadian Army in World War I and was appointed Canadian Government representative at the front in 1916.

Beaverbrook was strongly criticized by part of the Establishment for his attitude to Lord Mountbatten and the Duke of Edinburgh.

It is probable that Beaverbrook's opposition to these two royal gentlemen was too extreme. But he was all-out, never half-hearted in his political affairs. And his quarrel with them was political. Every punch was aimed for a knock-out. Some punches may have fallen low. His guard was often open to counter-attack. He struck to wound and was unafraid to bleed. That was his weakness—and his strength.

The legend of the man's crudity and coarseness is a lie. In an age where bad manners have become smart, Beaverbrook remained one of the most courteous of men. The wife of a Cabinet Minister met him not long before he died. She said afterwards, 'I expected somebody rough-hewn. I met a man with the exquisite and sensitive ways of a Victorian gentleman at his best.'

Sometimes Beaverbrook suffered from gout. It is a painful affliction which causes depression in its cure as well as its onset. But when free from gout, Beaverbrook rose to his feet each time any lady came into the room, and would remain standing till she was seated. At eighty-four he still insisted, rain or shine, wet or fine, on accompanying his guests to the door of his home when they left him, and bidding them 'God-speed' on their way.

The startling truth about Beaverbrook is that he happened to be a very nice man. Nothing stung his enemies more or surprised those who talked much of him but knew him slightly than this view of him. His shouting and bullying, his extravagant postures and the violence of his warfare were all overcoats protecting a spirit exceedingly sensitive to the cold winds and warmer airs of life. Sensitive, too, in an amazing way to the things that were happening the other side of the hill, the troubles and joys in another human heart.

During my last visit to my old friend I read him the sentences with which I proposed to end this book:

'Beaverbrook is far from the adventurer that his enemies like to describe and denounce. He has in him the stuff which through history some great saints and great sinners have shared. Its name is compassion.

'But compassion is not enough. Capacity for friendship is not enough. The pomp of human power which he craves, the art of controlling the destiny of men and nations which he quests—these things are not enough.

'One thing is lacking. And in the heart of him Beaverbrook knows it is the one thing that counts. It is the truth of the gospel that his father preached in those far-off childhood days. It is surrender to the full claim of Christ which he has always known, always resisted, and which still bears constantly upon him.

'There is an old hymn:

> When the harvest is past and the summer is o'er,
> And Jesus invites us no more.

'He has waited long enough now.

'I hope and fight and pray that he does not wait too long. 'The harvest may be past if he waits much longer.'

Lord Beaverbrook was silent. He looked at me for a long time. He then said, 'Peter, that is right'.

It remains my conviction that he did not wait too long. And his spirit rejoices in the dignity and love of his son, Max Aitken, who renounced the title Beaverbrook with the words, 'Certainly in my lifetime there will only be one Lord Beaverbrook'.

15

EPILOGUE

MAX was master of words. But words mean little in writing about my old master after he has gone into silence. There are things to be said which cannot yet be said.

This book was finished when he was alive. It was with the publisher when he died. There are passages in it which for the sake of accuracy or from risk of libel he had to see. His comment was, 'My God, Peter, you're rough on me. But it's the truth.'

Here is the tribute of someone who loved him as he was but strove for years without power or influence but with hope and vision to help him become the man he could, and should have been.

It is a tribute to the unknown Max, who, underneath the might and money, loved life and his family and his friends like a boy. He was a boy who won every prize with the skill of his hand and the sharpness of his sword. No trophy was given him without a struggle. He attacked an establishment that never accepted him. He was easily hurt, often hurt, and hated being hurt, but would scorn to admit it. Sometimes he had the heedless cruelty of a boy taking revenge when harm is done him. Always he showed the uncalculated compassion of a child for others when they were in trouble. In youth, he bet his life against the full claim of his father's faith. In age, he began to wonder whether he had lost that bet. Secretly, he began to hedge it.

He was the best journalist of our times. The world asks whether the *Express* newspapers will now maintain their flair. The answer is *yes*. Years ago Beaverbrook said to me of someone who left him, 'He does not understand the paper is bigger than him'. Beaverbrook punched his mark on his newspapers. But they are bigger than Beaverbrook. They will continue to infuriate—and flourish. His son and heir, Max, with his colleagues will perpetuate the pepper, and quarry the news which has built their circulation.

A few days before he died Beaverbrook made a speech at a party given in his honour by his fellow-Canadian and friend, Lord Thomson of Fleet. Alas, I was not bidden to the banquet. But I watched on television. Max Beaverbrook ended, 'This is my final word. It is time for me to become an apprentice once more. I have not settled in which direction. But somewhere, sometime soon. . . .' On his return home, he fell ill and shortly departed.

He is now an apprentice in Heaven. He will express surprise at finding the late Lord Baldwin there. He will not, I fancy, resist too strongly the temptation to try and rob his old adversary of some of the charms of that place. When the Great Umpire shouts 'No', apprentice Max will still, with a grin, dispute the Umpire's decision. But he will find the Almighty more charitable than his earthly critics. The man's faults and follies were known to millions and broadcast by a host of antagonists. His virtues were many, but known to few.

On his birthday each year, 25 May, I would send him a verse or two of fun and affection. On his last birthday on earth, a few days before he died, I struck a more serious note.

When the Last Edition goes to press and all the news is told,
And what was said or done counts more than countless copies sold,
When all the lies that seemed the truth are shining in the light,
And all the truth, now hidden, by the Reader brought to sight,

Your valour, Max, and vision by smaller men decried,
As Front Page news will hit the eye, not tucked away inside—
The story of a boy whose hands in history played a part,
With Black Ink running in his veins and Empire in his heart.

But more than this. A man whose sword, drenched with the blood of life,
Slept never, failed yet fought again, unsheathed and sharp with strife.
A man, whatever sins there be, whose love was always great,
Whose laughter never let his foes lower him into hate.
A man who in the pomp of power, the blaze of gold and glory,
Gambling with greatness, never could forget the greatest story.
The Last Edition gives the news, purged from all sham and dross,
Of Max, the true, the real Max with his Master at the Cross.